My
PERFECT
PLACE
in
SCOTLAND

My PERFECT PLACE *in* SCOTLAND

Personalities share their most-loved locations

Edited by
Sally Magnusson

Photography by Susie Lowe

BLACK & WHITE PUBLISHING

First published in the UK in 2023 by
Black & White Publishing Ltd
Nautical House, 104 Commercial Street, Edinburgh, EH6 6NF

A division of Bonnier Books UK
4th Floor, Victoria House, Bloomsbury Square, London, WC1B 4DA
Owned by Bonnier Books
Sveavägen 56, Stockholm, Sweden

This collection edited by and copyright © Sally Magnusson 2023
Individual chapters © the Contributors 2023
Project editor: Rachel Morrell

A CIP catalogue record for this book is available from the British Library.

ISBN: 978 1 78530 483 5

1 3 5 7 9 10 8 6 4 2

Layout by Black & White
Printed and bound in Lithuania

FSC
www.fsc.org

MIX
Paper from
responsible sources
FSC® C107574

www.blackandwhitepublishing.com

Nae day sae dark; nae wüd sae bare;
Nae grund sae stour wi' stane;
But licht comes through; a sang is there;
A glint o' grass is green.

William Soutar (1898 – 1943)

CONTENTS

INTRODUCTION

It's a privilege to have had a hand in fashioning this beautiful book. I hope reading it and swooning over the photographs brings you as many hours of pleasure as editing the text has given me.

Here is Scotland in all its glorious diversity: from the Eildon Hills in the Borders to Badachro in the north-west and Brora in Sutherland; from the grassy-duned beaches of Fife to the sands of Camusdarach on the opposite coast; from the secret paths of a Perthshire hotel to a kitchen table in the heart of Glasgow.

Here you'll find all kinds of people from different areas of life sharing their connection to one little patch of Scottish earth. Unique though each experience may be, what these thoughtful and honest accounts reveal is how much it matters to everyone to have a place where the deepest parts of us can be nourished. A place to bathe in memories and make new ones. A place to discover wisdom, and perspective, and sometimes good food. A place for fun. A place to be happy. A place, above all, where we can truly be ourselves.

People muse in these pages about nature and our responsibility for it; about the importance of leaving the phone behind; about the calming effect – on minds sometimes tightened to snapping point by the unremitting stresses of modern life – of being in the presence of wind and wave or hill and sky, of taking the time to wonder at the pollen parcels on a bee's leg or listen to water coursing along a stony burn.

It is no coincidence that SAMH, the Scottish Association for Mental Health, is the book's partner. Mental health, and the role of place in helping to sustain it, is the drumbeat beneath much that is shared here.

The great thing is that it's not only Scotland's wild spaces and extravagant beauties that bestow such rootedness and joy. Some people find their perfect place in the noise and bustle of community, whether eating Indian food around a table in Leith or delighting in the smell of chips and petrol fumes in Paisley. Another finds perfection in being at home in Argyll in the company of two beloved dogs.

This is a book full of warmth and surprises. I hope you love it.

Sally Magnusson

CHRIS HOY

CRAIGLOCKHART HILL

CHRIS HOY is an internationally renowned cyclist with six Olympic gold medals, one silver medal and eleven world championship victories. In 2008 he became the first British athlete in a hundred years to win three gold medals in a single Olympic games. Since retiring from cycling, he has developed his own range of kids' bikes, won the 2015 European Le Mans motorsport series and written multiple books. He also hosts the podcast *Sporting Misadventures*. Chris was awarded a knighthood in 2008 and is an ambassador for SAMH and UNICEF UK among other charities.

My perfect place is Craiglockhart Hill in Edinburgh. I used to go there a lot when I was younger, particularly in my teenage years and into my twenties. Happy memories draw us towards them and this is a place where I had so much fun.

There are various different paths up there, and the walk to the top is all part of the fun. There's a gentle, gradual path you can take, but in those days we used to clamber straight up the steep ones. Whichever way you go, it only takes a few minutes to get from being right in the hub of the city with all the shops, the buses and the people, to being high up and away from it all. You have a bit of time to sit and think and look all the way out to the Forth Rail Bridge, all the way across the town, all the way to the castle. It's a wonderful way to look at a beautiful city.

You see a huge mixture of people walking their dogs, exercising, going for a wander. There's all kinds. And it's free. It's one of those now rare things you can do that is fun and doesn't cost anything, which is important in life and was especially so for me as a teen.

Life in those teenage years tends to be about your friendship group. It's that time before you're old enough to go out to the pubs but don't want to be sitting at home with your mum and dad. You can't loiter on the street corners either, so it's often difficult to find somewhere to go.

Luckily for us, Craiglockhart Hill fulfilled that role. In my mid-teens, I had a friend who lived up near Craiglockhart sports centre and introduced us to the hill. Although we weren't really interested in the view, we quickly decided this was a cool place to go. It became a social spot to watch the sunset and play music on our little ghetto blaster.

One of our favourites was an Edinburgh pirate radio station called Boomerang FM. They would be on air for a few weeks in a row then disappear. So on Friday evenings we'd sit there with the radio trying to find the frequency, because it wasn't always the same. You'd be just tuning and waiting, then all of a sudden stumble across it on a random frequency and, "Oh, we found it!" Boomerang FM got a lot of airtime up the hill, along with whatever tape each of us had brought along. We'd listen to The Stone Roses, The Charlatans, a fair mixture of tastes. Whenever I hear any of these songs today,

it takes me straight back to those times. It's so wonderful to have places that make you happy and bring back your memories.

Later, when I was competing in cycling and would come back to Edinburgh to see the family, I would somehow end up on Craiglockhart Hill again. Before I left for the 2000 Olympics in Sydney, I came home for about two days, literally, just to see my folks and to pick up some stuff. I really didn't have time, but I dashed up the hill anyway and just sat there.

And there you are, looking out on the lights and the bustling and the cars. There are all those people you can't see but know are there, all those thousands living lives that you don't know any-

thing about. It makes you realise that actually what you're doing – even if it's the Olympics – is quite a small, insignificant thing.

Stepping back and seeing the bigger picture like this is a very calming and centring thing to do, especially when you're worrying about something and it's easy to blow things out of proportion. Looking back now, I realise that being on the hill gave me perspective.

It's important to recognise the significance of a place where you can reset and reflect and gain perspective. When I began going up Craiglockhart Hill for my own pleasure, it was before there was any discussion about mental health. Even in 2008, when I became an ambassador for the mental health charity SAMH at a time when they were really struggling, nobody was talking about it. Mental health was a taboo subject.

It came to my own attention because of the Scottish cyclist Graeme Obree, who, despite having no coaching team or entourage, became a world champion in the mid-nineties. He didn't have anything on his side apart from his genius, his work ethic, his friends and a very supportive wife. He built a bike with his own two hands, using scrap metal and bearings from an old washing machine, because he couldn't afford to buy one. Then he basically invented a new riding position on the bike and went on to be a world champion and record holder, and to do everything I dreamed of in cycling.

When I heard this amazing story as a teenager, Graeme Obree became my absolute inspiration and hero. I imagined that if you had all that, you'd be getting up every morning with a big smile on your face, completely happy to know that everything was great. That's what I thought until I got to know him.

Graeme's final world championships were my first, and we shared a room. I think our coach knew I was a massive fan, so he put us together. As we talked, it transpired that Graeme had had mental health problems his whole life and had attempted suicide on a number of occasions. I realised then that success didn't equal happiness. It was horrible to think that if Graeme felt like this and managed to hide it, there must be many people in similar positions who weren't seeking help.

Although I was fortunate in not having any mental health problems myself, over the years I could see numerous friends, teammates and even family members who had struggled without anyone knowing what it was or what to do about it. So becoming an ambassador for SAMH was really something I did for Graeme and people like him. I'm very proud to have played a small role in raising awareness and support for this cause over the past fifteen years.

You think about how much has changed since then. Mental health is right at the top of the agenda now, which is great, although the reason we're discussing it is because it's grown into such a huge issue. Now that we are more conscious of it, I hope there's a better chance that people will recognise when things aren't going so well and reach out for support.

Life is so busy and we're always trying to cram so much into it. It's very human to have times we want to be around people and equally times when we need space and perspective. That's when it's important to have these places that can give a bit of distance, a bit of physical space and head space too. Somewhere we can step back and just enjoy the view.

As I've grown older, what Craiglockhart Hill means to me has changed. At one time it was all about bringing music and having fun. Then it became a place to reflect. Now I'm looking forward to taking my kids there and making more memories for the future.

The last time I went up Craiglockhart Hill, I was visiting Edinburgh for an event and realised I had time on my hands. I had planned to go to a coffee shop and look at my phone, but I just thought, *Wait a minute – there's nothing to stop me.* This time I wasn't climbing up the steep banks with muddy knees and elbows. I just took the gentle path, alone, and it felt really nice. Now I'm thinking about it, I need to get back up there again.

LAURA YOUNG

CAMUSDARACH BEACH

LAURA YOUNG is a climate activist and ethical influencer from Glasgow. Under the name Less Waste Laura she became a social media sensation in 2018 with her campaign to reduce waste. She is a regular contributor for the BBC and Sky News, and spoke at TedX Glasgow in 2019. Laura has received many awards for her work, including Scottish Influencer of the Year in the Inspiration category (2022) and Climate Creator to Watch (2023).

My perfect place is a beach on the north-west coast of Scotland – Camusdarach Beach, which is just south of Mallaig, just north of Arisaig. The seashore scenes in the Scottish movie *Local Hero* were filmed there in the eighties. It's a stunning location which looks totally different depending on the time of day or time of year. It's peaceful. It's rugged. It's moody. It's beautiful.

There's this one bit particularly that always takes my breath away. To get to the beach there's a short path, maybe only a few hundred metres long. But you're winding down this little sandy path, knowing that you're heading towards the beach. On either side you've got different Scottish plants. You've got ferns, you've got bluebells in May, and there are bright yellow flowers – "whins" we call them in Scotland. You're winding down this path and you can hear the ocean. And as you

walk down, the path grows sandier and sandier until you eventually pop out right into this small dune.

As you turn the corner, you're exposed to this huge landscape, where, on a clear day, you can see the isles of Eigg, Rum and Skye. Some days there's turquoise water and blue skies and white sandy beaches: a breathtaking view. But on other days you come round the corner and just get smacked in the face with a big gust of wind. Or it's raining and you can't see any islands. There's a surprise waiting every time. Whenever I bring people to my perfect place, I'm always like, *Just wait, just wait, just wait.* I almost want to run ahead to see what they look like when they get to it.

Growing up, my family went on holidays to Scottish places, and quite often we would go to the Highlands. I grew up in Glasgow without that kind of coastal environment and so I always wanted to spend my free time on the beach. Now that I've discovered this one, I take any chance I get to come up and visit – even just to work from here. At five o'clock, I close my laptop, run for the beach and go swimming.

My mum had already taken me on a few hill walks, but doing the Duke of Edinburgh Award at school gave me a passion for being outside. So on these holidays around Scotland, no matter the circumstances, I'd be going on walks, cycling, swimming, or on the beach.

I think I always knew that I wanted my career to be something to do with the

environment, but I didn't know what it would look like.

There was an important moment when I was in my final year of university. Our family had come up here for Hogmanay and we went on a New Year's Day walk along the beach. Everyone was talking about resolutions. I didn't really know what the year would bring, but I wanted to pick something to challenge myself with and keep me focused.

As we were doing this, we walked further and further along the beach and kept coming across litter. Crisp packets or fishing line – no matter what it was, we kept finding it. Eventually my hands were so full that I realised I actually couldn't

pick it all up. So I thought, *This is what I could do.*

I suppose that's where Less Waste Laura was born. All my work and campaigning has basically grown out of that moment. It wasn't exactly a lightbulb moment, because I knew before then that I cared, but that was when I decided to do something, and after that I started speaking out online.

When your work is dedicated to something like environmental sustainability or climate change, I think it's important to look at the small wins. All justice issues are huge and they won't be solved with one decision. So that's why my work focuses on the tangible things we can do and the

conversations we can have. It's about the journey rather than the end point: to look at some of the changes that we can see and achieve collectively.

Then, at other times, the work grows a little bigger, like a staff campaign to divest our pensions and a campaign to ban disposable vapes. Even if the high point of success is when they actually get banned, we reached those small goals along the way too.

The biggest thing we're fighting is misinformation. I think most people agree that it's good to try and care for the environment. But the way we go about it creates debate. Often we get so lost in the detail that we forget to take a step back

"Often we get so lost in the detail that we forget to take a step back and paint a picture of what we could create."

"It's about joining a local wildlife
group, getting involved in a community
garden, physically seeing the changes
in front of you."

and paint a picture of what we could create and the kind of sustainable environment we want.

I'll constantly be in conversations where people ask which is better – a petrol car that lasts fifteen to twenty years, or an electric car that's got a battery, or a diesel car. Well, the best thing is a bus (affordable and accessible) or a train, a bike or walking. If you don't have a car but do have plenty of ways to get around, what you actually have is a beautiful world.

All my memories include terrible images like the skinny polar bear on an ice cap, so it feels normal to worry about the environment. One of the things I do struggle with, though, is fighting apathy. As a young person, you know, you can feel really empowered among your own peers. You'll find consensus, passion, ability – but not necessarily influence. It can be frustrating, thinking if we only had the votes or the positions in power or the finances, we'd be able to shift things.

I fight by getting involved, keeping busy. It's about joining a local wildlife group, getting involved in a community garden, physically seeing the changes in front of you. I'm a Christian, and my faith is a big part of my activism. Praying about these issues is part of my hope. I love working with Christians and other faith groups to be like, *Come on, let's do this*.

When COP26 was coming to Glasgow, I was rallying all these churches to become involved and that was powerful. Afterwards, my church planted a mini-wood. We ended up planting a whole orchard and wildflowers too.

It might not be to do with faith, but we can all be part of a community, can't we? Maybe you like looking at nature but not being in it. You might be good at graphic design, and you can make some cool infographics. Or you might be good at writing. Or you might be able to sit in a boardroom and do the finances because you're an accountant. It all counts.

It's also about recognising that our eco-anxiety is nothing compared to that of people who're experiencing climate change. We need to get our butts in gear, because they are having to move from places that are becoming uninhabitable, which then makes their livelihoods uncertain. So I'm going to speak to my councillors, and I'm going to write to my MP and my MSP, because even though we aren't seeing the drastic effects yet, other communities are. If we don't do something now, it will be too late.

Even in this area there were some really bad wildfires last year. I remember thinking, *This is exactly why we need to do something*. Wildfires can be good for some environments. But to know that, because of the dry weather, we've created this scorched land where it shouldn't be is heartbreaking. I've never turned up to my house to find it washed away by a flood, but that experience was like a tiny grain of sand, that feeling of, *Oh my gosh, I almost lost this place*. It's really special to me and lots of other people.

I travelled up to Camusdarach after the wildfires and I was driving past tree skeletons that looked like charcoal. It helped me to appreciate that environments we

love are just one moment away from disaster, whether it's a fire, or a flood, or even a lack of pollination through not treating our insects right. You realise every landscape is precious.

That's why it feels important for me to reconnect with nature when I'm working to save it. So often you're an eco-warrior in a room with a laptop. But as humans we need to reset and recharge, physically going back outside. Even the little green park next to my flat will do. I go there three times a day, and it's just this small thing to do, but I can sit in the grass and breathe for a minute.

And it has been nice recently, coming up to Camusdarach and seeing the plants return. Earth is resilient and it can heal if we help it. Seeing the bluebells and listening to the cuckoo birds – I love it. There's no signal and you can just put your feet in the ocean and let it come and wash away whatever you're thinking. It's such a relief.

SALLY MAGNUSSON

THE RED BURN

Sally Magnusson is an award-winning author, journalist and broadcaster. Her TV roles have included presenting the BBC's *Breakfast* programme, *Songs of Praise* and *Reporting Scotland*. Among her books are three acclaimed works of historical fiction and the *Sunday Times* non-fiction bestseller, *Where Memories Go*. After observing the effect of music on her mother's dementia, she founded the charity Playlist for Life and in 2023 was awarded an MBE for that work.

Every morning I do this. I grab my oldest jacket or, if it's wet outside, my 66° North waterproofs from Iceland – not the shop but my other homeland, where they know how to cater for rain, believe me. I call the dog and walk. Walk fast along the burn between the fields, revelling in the wildflowers along the verges, listening to the cries of sheep and the blethering of birds, gulping big lungfuls of air as I go and feeling immensely thankful – this is something I'm conscious of every single day – to be here in this unassumingly beautiful little patch of Scottish earth.

We live in a farmhouse in countryside just north of Glasgow. The house was long ago separated from ownership of the land around it, and today neighbouring farmers use the fields for grazing sheep ("wee yams" as my toddler grandson calls them) and cattle. Walking the paths beside the farmland is how I start the day. It's a loop that barely takes me out of sight of my own backyard and I love it.

It's not the escape from thought that I would maybe go looking for on holiday, along some windy beach or secluded loch. The opposite actually. This walk tends to be a time for active thinking, although it's the kind of thinking you get to do in peace before returning to a bleeping phone and a pile of emails and all the rest of it: decisions about what to wear for work, a toddler pouring plastic animals over the floor and yogurt over the new sofa, a man who's arrived to see about the boiler, last night's dishes eyeing you accusingly from the sink.

During the periods when I'm writing, I use the time for thinking about characters, plot or the novel's structure. There's a mental clarity that comes from striding out like this in the fresh air or the rain, even if the conclusions arrived at have precious little to do with my surroundings.

I remember on one of these morning walks realising all of a sudden that the little daughter of Ásta, my seventeenth-century Icelandic protagonist in *The Sealwoman's Gift*, would have to be sent to the Sultan's palace in Constantinople; at last I had my dramatic turning point. Another time, stomping up the farm hill while lambs clamoured for their breakfast, I found myself thinking about my great-grandmother, evicted from Mull in the Highland Clearances and trying to make a new life in a Glasgow tenement,

and there it was: the germ of the idea that became *Music in the Dark*.

Sometimes, I'm consciously taking note of feelings and observations as I go. My second novel, *The Ninth Child*, is set in the Trossachs in the 1850s, where the great Loch Katrine waterworks were being built in a landscape not unlike this one thirty miles away. As the book took shape, I thought very deliberately about that landscape on my walk. Rejoicing in the sting of rain, hurled about by wind, marvelling over the downy autumn softness of a thistle-head, I imagined that I was my sheltered, middle-class Victorian protagonist encountering nature for the first time, and the exhilaration of it all for a woman who had barely moved a muscle

in the city. Then I went straight home to write it.

I even wrote a series of children's books based on these very paths, these wild flowers, these birds, these shy rabbits that scatter when they see you, these secret lochans, these dusky woods. It became the territory of one Horace the Haggis, whose idyll was only spoiled by the vengeful presence of Farmer McPhee up the road. (And belated apologies here to my blameless neighbour William, who has never hurt a haggis in his life.)

Day by day, the seasons unfold around me as I walk. Daffodils and primroses in the spring, and the whiff of wild garlic in the wind. Violets clinging to the banks of the burn. Hawthorn trees foaming into creamy blossom. Sticky young leaves gleaming silver in the sunshine. Air smelling of earth, and manure, and the perfume of dog roses.

As summer goes on it's the sweetness of the wild lily that captures your senses as you pass. One side is a sea of thistles, the other a glory of buttercups and white clover. Ragged yellow heads of bird's-foot trefoil appear in the long grasses, and purple dots of self-heal. There are foxgloves beaded with rain, rowans preparing their berries. Swallows flit around in the breeze and settle on the phone lines.

In the autumn, mushrooms balloon from the earth and spiders thread nets of such

"Day by day, the seasons unfold
around me as I walk."

> "It's a lovely place to do what
> I so seldom do: stop."

pearly beauty among the gorse bushes that your heart catches and you wonder how on earth you can loathe spiders so much when they can produce something so lovely – which is a metaphor for much else in life when you think about it and the sort of thought you have time for on a walk like this.

As the year turns, it's ice time, the cold of it seeping deep into your bones and making your teeth ache. Frost scums the burn and turns the bare trees along the bank – willow, ash, sycamore – into spectral beings. Pale fog joins sky to field and everything becomes ghostly. You nearly jump out of your skin when a rook screeches suddenly into the quiet.

I don't think I ever sit down on this walk. Mostly that's because I'm nearly always late for something at the other end, but it's also because making it to the top of one (spectacularly modest) hill is the nearest I get to anything approaching aerobic exercise, and if I take a rest, I'm lost. To take my mind off the climb I'll usually turn to the previous day's episode of Radio 4's *The Archers*, which sees me nicely to the top. There are times when I haven't been sure whether the cows are

mooing through my earbuds or making a rumpus for real in the top field.

Some days I'll have time to take the path further round to what my children used to call, optimistically, the Waterfall, although it's really only the burn tumbling over a few stones and into a tiny pool. When they were young, we used to go there with a picnic – one of these Scottish excursions which are invariably more attractive in the imagining than the waspy, prickly-grass reality. The older ones would balance hazardously on the slippery stones, while I risked life and limb trying to keep the baby from disappearing downstream.

These days it's a lovely place to do what I so seldom do: stop. For a few moments I can stand on the little wooden bridge and let the sound of the water drown out everything else: news developments, writing ideas, plans for the day, reasons to get a move on.

Why is tumbling water so soothing? Maybe because it's on its way to some-where else. Just for a while, my lovely burn does the hurrying for me and I get to contemplate my perfect place while thinking of absolutely nothing else.

ANNA CAMPBELL-JONES

My Kitchen Table

———————————

ANNA CAMPBELL-JONES is an interior designer, broadcaster and influencer. She is a presenter and a judge on *Scotland's Home of the Year*. Anna owns the interior design company HABITUS and in 2022 she was awarded Scottish Influencer of the Year in the interiors and design category. Anna has built a reputation in the design community. Her work has been featured in several leading publications and showcases an exciting blend of old and new, re-purposing vintage pieces to create contemporary interiors.

As someone who is originally from London, making my home in Scotland was a definite choice. We visited a lot when I was younger, going far up north to Cape Wrath and to the islands of the west coast. But I had never been to Glasgow, and that was where one day I would find my perfect place.

It started with attending Glasgow School of Art. I grew up in a very modernist, minimalist space designed by my father, who was an architect. On a few occasions he would take me to sites, so I got to see the transformation of buildings. I found the mess made to create something beautiful so exciting. Back then, in the late eighties, interior design was a new degree and taught at very few places, so I applied to the only interior design course in Scotland, which was at Glasgow School of Art. I was a huge fan of Charles Rennie Mackintosh, and I loved the idea that you would be able to look across the street to his building.

When I stepped off the train, I was completely gobsmacked by how spectacular Central Station was. Even though it was early spring, there was this vivid blue sky and – in that beguiling way that Glasgow has – the sun was shining. I walked with my heavy portfolio up through all the amazing grandeur of the Victorian sandstone buildings. By the time I arrived at the art school, I was thinking, *I have to get in*. I was probably a little precocious and forthright in my interview, but I did get in. And that was the first step to making Scotland my home.

The second step came after art school, when the opportunity arose to relocate to Glasgow with my then husband, after a hard stint working and raising a baby in London. We wanted green spaces to bring children up in and could finally afford more than a one-bedroom flat. So we arranged surveys, made offers and fell in love with houses which then fell through. Until one day I came to view this place.

The front garden was like something out of *Sleeping Beauty*: you had to kind of double over to get through the undergrowth. I came through the gate to this thicket with a little pixie tunnel, shaped by a tiny lady in her nineties called Mrs Kilgour who had lived there whose – sometimes cheeky, always benign – presence we still feel to this day. I found my way to the front door and opened it to reveal this massive hallway. I asked the agent which way it was to the flat, and he said, "No, this *is* the flat." Before I'd even looked at the rooms, I was like, "This is it." It had quite a bit of fire damage, but finding a property, whether buying or renting, is a bit like dating: when you know, you know. Even if it's got short-comings, you forgive it.

In this flat there was absolutely nothing. No loo. The kitchen had a broken window and a pigeon lying on the floor. So we gutted the whole place. And now I would say that if I had to pick my favourite spot in the house, it would indeed be the kitchen.

I think a lot of people, myself included, have the most significant conversations of their lives sitting at the kitchen table. It's that moment, perhaps, where you've just finished eating or drinking and there's a space just hovering in time. There's no rush, so conversations can emerge, whether it's about the exciting thing you want to do in life or talking to children about their careers. It's a great place to share worries with the people you love, but it's also a place for ideas.

A friend of mine was sitting at the table once, and we were talking about products we would love to bring to people's homes. Over numerous cups of tea and home-made vegan rocky road, we hatched a plan to start a business. And we did. Even though I have my studio, I'll often bring my work to the kitchen, and we'll just sit in the sunshine thinking, *What shall we call it?* and *What's the domain name?*, and ideas flow in a very informal space.

My kitchen is rather quirky. The walls are a gorgeous bright green, which I think is quite jolly. When we moved in, I found a stainless-steel manufacturer and got them to weld me a worktop with all the appliances freestanding and a Marmoleum floor with welded seams. I was so used to designing for restaurants in Soho that rats were at the front of my mind at that time. The table and chairs were from Dad's architecture practice – I snaffled them when he retired. They've been through the wars, but I absolutely love them. He got the chairs out of a skip and had them rechromed and reupholstered back in the seventies. They date to the early 1930s and are really special, like family heirlooms that people have taken on after being thrown away.

Along with the furniture, Dad passed on the skip-diving mentality as well. I have a

"Home is where you make memories. They accumulate like barnacles, and that's what my kitchen is like."

big old dresser from a charity shop that I painted, and there's this orange Guzzini light over the table, which was from a skip too. Well, the original one was. It got broken and I've never known how, as to this day nobody has admitted to it. I thought it was an opportunity to change the look, but my kids insisted it had to be the same, this big orange glowing light in the centre of everything. It's a vintage sixties light, so it took me ages to find online. If that breaks, I'll need to build a storeroom full of them. But I understand why children don't want their parents' home to change. As soon as my children walk in, they're back in kid mode, and that's how it should be.

Home is where you make memories. They accumulate like barnacles, and that's what my kitchen is like. My stainless-steel worktop scratches from the moment you use it, but after a few years, it's just thousands and thousands of scratches, from opening a bottle of wine or dragging a food mixer over the counter, or cutting something on the surface when you're feeling lazy. Every scratch is there, from my kids standing on the counter making fairy cakes, to me cooking up something, which I absolutely love to do.

Still, this does all change. It's like rubbed-out words on a page, ready to be written on again but still bearing the indents.

At one point, the kitchen table was a place where I would feed the children before my husband would come home and clear everything away, and then one of us would cook again for the adults. After he left and it was just me and my two boys, I realised I wanted to eat with them. That was a big moment in my life, finding ways of cooking that my children would enjoy, that would nourish the three of us and help us to heal. The full range of life, everything that has happened to me, so much of it is in that room.

In my line of work, we think a lot about home and how we can help people to express their identity and find comfort in the space they live in. When you invite people in, you're inviting them into a version of yourself. It has objects, pictures, colours, things that tell the real story of you.

My kitchen now signifies contentment. I have exceptionally long Sunday breakfasts with my partner Peter, reading the papers from cover to cover and discussing the world. At the end of the day, my favourite moment is when I switch off the computer, go to the kitchen and start cooking. There's something so creative about choosing a dish and how you want to present your plate. Music goes on, I'll chop an onion, have a glass of wine and a little boogie. There's many a kitchen disco in my house nowadays. It's a lovely way to recalibrate your brain after a day of running around.

Setting everything straight and learning perspective: I have found that here. So of course it feels like my perfect place, and it always will. In fact, you'd have to drag me out of here.

JAMES COSMO

RIVER NITH

————————

JAMES COSMO is a renowned actor and producer from Dunbartonshire. James has appeared in over 130 films and many beloved television series. He is well-known for his roles in *Game of Thrones, Braveheart, Highlander, His Dark Materials* and *Trainspotting* and in 2018 was awarded an MBE for his work. In 2023 James achieved a lifelong dream and launched his own whisky, STORYMAN, created in a unique partnership with award-winning Annandale Distillery in Dumfries & Galloway.

My perfect place is not really a specific place at all. It's a river or a stream, and it can be anywhere. So if you fish the Nith or the Annan, one of the great Borders rivers, it's a delight. If you go to New Zealand and fish a river there, it's the same magical place where you can find solitude and peace. It's a state of mind.

I think I was genetically programmed to look for that. Before he became an actor, my father was a river warden on the Loch Lomond river system: the Ettrick, the Fruin, the Leven and, of course, Loch Lomond. When I was a little boy, I used to dream of fishing. As I started to read for enjoyment, the main books I read were all about fly fishing. Every single one. I knew exactly where I wanted to be and that was beside the stream, looking at the water.

The first place I fished was the River Leven, right in the middle of Dumbarton. A delightful stretch, just delightful. It was called the Slaughterhouse and I used to fish there with my friend Eddie. We caught a lot there, before I really got into fly fishing properly.

Fly fishing is very much a zen thing. You concentrate on something so precisely. You've sat in your living room or hut and tied a tiny little fly under the magnifying glass and put it on the hook. Come spring, you go out and you see a trout rising somewhere and you cast that fly out as gently as you can. You see little rises in the water, you know, like the streams coming down here and there. A trout is over there but it isn't by a rock; the rock is here. And the water comes down the rock and the real flies get pushed up. So I've got to put my fly in there and he'll be sitting behind that rock waiting to come get them.

"And if something interrupts you, well, maybe it's a kingfisher, an otter or a butterfly. I mean, what can be more beautiful than that?"

A river is a bit like staring at a fire – there's something hypnotic about it. All those small eddies of the water, little bits of foam, the edges of the water pushing the trotters to the top. It's like saying a mantra in your head, because everything else in your mind disappears. All your worries, all your concerns. The only thing you're thinking about is that fly and waiting for that fish, because if you miss, when that fish comes up, it's gone.

It is very much an exercise in meditation. I often go fishing for the day and don't catch anything. But you've still had a great day's fishing; I've still been out there. And if something interrupts you, well, maybe it's a kingfisher, an otter or a butterfly. I mean, what can be more beautiful than that? You come back realising that you've experienced peace of mind for eight hours.

I've read somewhere that there are different stages of a fisherman. The first one, you want to catch a fish. Then you want to catch the most fish. Then you want to catch the biggest fish. And then you just want to fish – you're not bothered. And it's true. When I started, I just wanted to catch a fish.

So we used what was called a "flying maggot". You'd catch a sea trout and it was always such a joy. We lived in a tenement at that time, so we knew the lady next door and the lady downstairs. You would just get a couple of trout and hang them on the door handle for their tea and that was always a lovely feeling.

You know, I don't even like the taste of trout, but I love catching them. With salmon, when that fly floats in front of their nose, it's only an annoyance, so they just snap at it and continue. But a trout, it lives in the river and it's feeding all the time, so it's wearier. It's looking at the thing that floats above it, thinking, *Does that look like the other flies?* So you've got to identify the kind of fly that's actually falling in the water. All through the year it's all different, so you have to choose wisely.

So it's much more of a contest with trout, although, as I say, I was never a lover of the taste. It had to be smoked or something, as it's quite a bland fish.

I shoot a lot as well and you've got to make use of something if you're to take it home. If you get a pheasant in the winter, you can take the feathers and use them to tie a fly, and you can use that fly to catch a trout in the summer. It's circular. But if you don't like the taste of something particularly and you don't have a hungry family to feed, well, put it back. He'll come back again and see you next year. He'll get bigger next year, and you'll have more fun.

I was fishing in Washington State with my friend Bo once, and I caught a king salmon. It was still alive when we put it in the net and weighed it. Thirty-two pounds it was, a huge fish. Bo said, "Well, James, it's the day before the season opens for king salmon. If we take this fish and go

back to the car and fishing game-catchers see us, we'll lose the car and all our equipment. What do you think we should do?"

I looked at this fish. I so wanted to have it on my wall somewhere. But I said, "Well, Bo, we'd better put him back." So we took a photograph and off he went.

Now I always use barbless hooks and let them go back in the river. It wasn't really a conscious decision to start freeing the fish. It's like that story of the Chinese philosopher who went fishing and eventually thought he wouldn't have a barb on his hook and took it off, because catching fish was, well, it's a feeling.

Someone said years ago that the days spent fly fishing are not counted in the lifetime of a man. God doesn't look down and say, "That was a day you had." He says, "No, that's okay." The more you can go fishing, the better it is for you. And God, He doesn't count it.

In the modern world, we're bombarded on all sides by social media, all those things which have no validity and cause a lot of mental health issues. To take yourself away from that and not be afraid of solitude is important. Because when you're alone and you've spent time being part of God's creation in the world, you return to society with a greater appreciation of your loved ones and other people. We notice how small we are, and how reliant on whatever we believe in to care for us. Being in nature gives us a sense of our place in the universe.

That's why I've always loved being in the Borders. The nature is so different to the ruggedness of the Highlands and the majesty of those mountains. Here, it's rolling hills and farmland and beautiful streams, and tiny trout-filled brooks.

It's a strange serendipity that one of my great heroes is Robert Burns. To be here within walking distance of his farm near Dumfries is extraordinary, and the fact that he knew the site which would become Annandale Distillery, where I'm creating my Storyman whisky, means a great deal to me too.

We have, of course, many great poets in the United Kingdom. But no one has had as much influence on the world with the sentiments that Burns expressed, at a time when those thoughts weren't accepted by everyone. I always feel so privileged just to look at the same views he did and breathe this same air. He was a wonderful, wonderful example of humanity.

I saw Cat Stevens being interviewed once and he said something regarding his conversion to Islam that was very brave at that time. He said he realised that life isn't a race and the richest man in the graveyard isn't the winner. I really took that to heart. Live the life you're going to live and don't live it for other people. Live the life you've been given: it's not up to anyone else to tell you how. Take time to look after yourself and find happiness within.

And the place where I find that happiness is on a river, gazing at water.

TONY SINGH

LEITH WALK

TONY SINGH is an award-winning chef who promotes Scottish produce in his multicultural dishes. He was awarded an MBE in 2017 for services to the food and drink industry and his restaurant Tony's Table earned a Michelin Bib Gourmand. Tony now runs a supper club in his home alongside the popular street food restaurant Radge Chaat and starred in *The Incredible Spice Men* alongside regular appearances on shows including *The Great British Menu*, *Saturday Kitchen* and *The One Show*.

Looking down Leith Walk in Edinburgh, I know I'm home. All around here is where I grew up.

Right at the top was my gran's house. We stayed in Tennant Street first, before it got knocked down. At the time it was called the Khyber Pass, where a lot of Indian and Irish families lived. That was right next to the vinegar factory, so it was bogging. After that, we lived near Smith's Place at the foot of the Walk, right across from the Volunteer Arms, locally called "The Volly". Then we moved to Cambridge Avenue, just off Balford Street. As a child walking up and down Leith Walk to visit Gran, there was a minefield of dog poo. Thankfully that's changed.

In those days, there were about thirty-two pubs on Leith Walk. Wherever you see a coffee shop or a restaurant today, there used to be a pub. There was one over the bus depot on stilts; it was wild. The shops have changed too. Then there were independent tailors, cobblers and bakers. On a Wednesday, everyone knew it was a half day and everything used to shut.

It's great to see all these areas, which were quite rough, changing. Some people say it's gentrified. Well, fantastic. Would you rather have fourteen different places to get coffee or a hammer attack? I'll take the coffee – fourteen cups please. You'll always have growing pains, but it's the right time. The street food, the independent brewers, the upcyclers, the artists . . . what hasn't changed is the craftspeople. The shoe shop was run by four generations. You had Brown's and the engineering works: things like that have always been there. It's just the next level. You've got a move from the old-school,

"The motto of Leith is 'Persevere'.
The people are grafters, with a few
scallywags mixed in as well"

family-owned businesses which spanned generations, to the new ones coming in and the tram system bringing people. But hopefully these new businesses will be handed down in the same way as before.

Leith only became part of Edinburgh in the 1920s, and it's always had a very independent identity, as all ports do. The motto of Leith is "Persevere". The people are grafters, with a few scallywags mixed in as well. But if you're a Leither, you're a Leither. It doesn't matter what age you are, what you've done or what you look like.

I'm third-generation Indian, but my family has a mix of heritage. My dad is from a village in India called Ghaloteia. My mum

was born in Glasgow. Her parents came over in the 1940s. I always felt part of the Sikh community, but we were very much taken in by everyone around us. There was a lot of racism at the time, but if it was kicking off, they had your back. It's a melting pot here, a place where you can integrate. There's a sense of community, a sense of right. I love to see my kids living in a place that's even more diverse, more welcoming.

My granny was the one who introduced me to cooking. The communal kitchen, the langar, is a cornerstone of the Sikh faith. We used to sit with a big pot of rice or lentils and pick through it, getting any nasty bits out before it got washed. It was like the first Tetris. I used to sit there for

ages, and I learned pretty quickly that if you helped out in the kitchen, you got to lick the spoon. Then the whole family sits down. It's all vegetarian and open to anybody. There's a lovely equality to the whole thing, and I think food is such a great vehicle if you want to break bread with somebody.

My first experience of cooking outside the house was at a restaurant called Le Monde on Thistle Street. There was a fantastic chef there who did home-cooked, traditional food, which I thought was amazing. I also worked at a casino at night when I was getting my diploma, so I could save up and buy records. I remember sneaking in with a white label record by Public Enemy, when my dad walked in. I said to him, "Just heading out to college," and in my rush to get out the door, I dropped the LP and ended up with a huge scratch across the front. I was heartbroken. Gutted. My dad never even realised; he had no idea. And that was the way it was at the time for me and everyone I knew: all our parents were quite strict and traditional, but we did get away with some things.

After my diploma, I went to chef college and it was all French, classical stuff and I thought, *Wow!* It really spurred me on to learn more. I had to persevere to make it through college for my core training as a chef, and it was hard. There were a lot of scary types in the kitchen. You had the head chef, sous chef, chef tournant, chef

de partie, first commis, second commis and so on.

I always wanted to put a twist on the food, but back then it was very strict, and as a young chef you couldn't try anything. I didn't train with Indian food. I was classically trained, and I loved learning haute cuisine. What I know about Indian food is all from my parents and grand-parents, but putting a spin on local food was always on my mind. You can't have all these wonderful flavours and not use them. When I got my own restaurant, it all took off and I got to cook for kings, queens, maharajas, you name it. People thought it wouldn't work, but it was that motto "Persevere" again. Now you see restaurants with Michelin stars and influences from all around the world, and I know why. It brings people and cultures together and tastes great.

That emphasis on hospitality and bring-ing people together round a table is why I started my Supper Club. We were thinking about another restaurant before lockdown; then I realised I wanted some-thing that created a sense of community. We started doing it every week. People are always nervous when they come to the house, but everyone mixes – old, young, couples – and it becomes this old-school dinner party. We've made so many connections. Some people were married in the same church or had been to the same school, but they'd never met each other before. It's such a relaxed and dif-ferent vibe that they all find themselves bonding.

The community aspect of Leith and my culture has taught me the importance of gathering with old friends and making new ones. It has always grounded me too. Success can turn your head, but here you've got a place and friends who will wind your neck right back round again. Walking up and down Leith Walk still feels fantastic, seeing people with their families and realising that the community is still going. You're always only a step away from someone you know or something to remind you of the past. Look down from Calton Hill and you realise the memories are as strong as ever.

EDDI READER

ROUKEN GLEN PARK

EDDI READER is an award-winning singer-songwriter. She first became famous as lead vocalist for the band Fairground Attraction before moving on to a solo career, reaching number 4 in the UK album chart with her 1994 album *Eddi Reader.* In 2003 she recorded *Eddi Reader Sings the Songs of Robert Burns,* to great critical acclaim. Eddi is the recipient of three Brit awards and was awarded an MBE in 2006 for her services to music.

Rouken Glen Park, to the south-west of Glasgow, is a fairy tale of a place for me. It's where my imagination first took wing as a child and I was able to dream of possibilities I couldn't see in the world around me.

At the time, we were living in a ground-floor tenement flat in Carnwadric, Arden. Our previous home was a tenement in Anderston, but then the M8 motorway was built and demolished everything in its path, including our home.

Our flat in Carnwadric had a little front garden bit, and a back court that everybody used. I remember going there with my little sister Jean and baby sister Barbara when I was five or six. We soon discovered that it was quite an aggressive area, with older boys going around in gangs and women who looked as if they would slice you from ear to ear. There

were men beating up women and fighting in the street. But beyond that there were exciting areas to explore, and that's how we found Rouken Glen Park.

Connecting to our council estate was a bit of "spare groun", as they called it, with old pianos and cars that people lit on fire. Beyond that was a little burn, where you would find baggy minnows and frogs and newts. Then, through a hole in the iron railing, there was a way up to lots of little businesses: a marble factory, and a tyre factory, which would also catch fire and create the most god-fearing cloud above your head that billowed dark grey and black. After that was a forest where I think they used to do army manoeuvres in the war. It had caves and a shaft someone could easily fall down, alongside a run of broken, derelict cottages, one of which we thought was a witch's hut. Then – if you managed to get just beyond that, crossing

"The park really was like
something out of a fairy tale. It was
full of beautiful waterfalls, tadpoles,
trees, lovely birds."

the dangers of Thornliebank Road – you hit the back of Rouken Glen Park.

The park really was like something out of a fairy tale. It was full of beautiful waterfalls, tadpoles, trees, lovely birds. It felt like a no-go area, because we'd sneaked through the fence from our poor part of town. But if you could get to the front gate, there was a massive Clydesdale horse that would pull you in a tram all the way up to the boating pond for tuppence. I imagined the park was full of princes, as everyone seemed to live in a castle.

Those folk stories, especially *Snow White and the Seven Dwarfs*, had a massive effect on me at that time, with the singing and the beauty of the forest. In the summer, you'd watch lovers winching and have your picnic that Mum would give you: a banana sandwich, then a packet of crisps and a drink of ginger. There were also the ordinary bits of the park, where you could play on the swings and all that, but I was much more interested in what my imagination would invent for me.

We found this waterfall with lots of coins in it, and someone told us you had to make a wish every time you passed it on the tiny bridge. We thought it was a troll bridge, where the three Billy Goats Gruff would walk across with a monster underneath. We frightened ourselves silly going across it.

I used to earn some money from babysitting, so I'd have money for some sweets and to go on the boats in the park, which we loved, but I'd save a tiny bit just for a wish. We'd go to the wishing fountain, which is what we always called the waterfall. That water was just a joy, the way it gushed in a magical way. My wishes were always about being happy and seeing the world, like my dad, who travelled all over the place as a contract welder.

It was really an escape to go to Rouken Glen Park and get away from babysitting and all the little ones. (We soon learned that every time my father came home from his travels, there would be a new sister or brother arriving a few months later.) By the pool, I thought I was some sort of mermaid, a magical being who could fly or Snow White hiding from the witch. Playing the part of Snow White running through the forest was special, because even though she's running, she's totally free.

By the age of eleven, I was turning into a five-foot-ten-and-a-half girl who was very long and clumsy. I was like Alice in Wonderland after she'd eaten the "make me bigger" thing. Our house was just too small and my sibling list was growing too. After me, Jean and Barbara came Danny. After Danny came Frank, then after Frank came Laura. I would commandeer the only space, which was either the bathroom or the press in the hall, chuck out all my dad's tools and sit with the guitar for hours until there was a bathroom queue a mile long.

Three years later, we came home from school and there was my mum, knitting. I asked, "What are you crocheting, Mum?" And she said, "It's for a new baby."

The last one, my youngest sister Richeal, was coming, and we realised the flat was just too small. So Mum began fervently trying to get a new house. Eventually, we went to Bourtreehill in Irvine, which was a big sprawling estate but quiet and beautiful.

The air was lovely there, near the glittering sea, so I could continue my fantasy life, looking at the waves coming in. Being in Ayrshire, Irvine also gave me access to music outside my own culture. I kind of

expanded, enjoying myself with all the musicians of the planet. In Glasgow, it was much more about a radical working-class revolution. But in Irvine, the music and focus were more pastoral and much more about the beauty in the land of Robert Burns and the beauty of love.

As Richard Brown said to Robert Burns, "Take your heart from the willow." When people hide their light, it can be described as putting your heart away into the willow tree, but you have to shake yourself out of it and not have anything to do with life's limitations. Just share a little light you feel is worth sharing. So that's what I did. Took my heart from my Scottish willow and decided to travel.

I first got the idea of a wider world from my dad. Sometimes, when he'd been working in the Highlands, he would bring us back the language of the north. "*Ciamar a tha sibh?*" he'd say in Gaelic and hold up a big lobster he'd dragged all the way home in a rickety car. I thought, *Wow, they have different languages out there*. It fuelled my wanderlust, the possibilities that the world could bring me.

I'd noticed pop and punk bands going down to London, but I was never attracted to that. I couldn't quite get my head around London being a glittering prize: it seemed quite dismal. On the other hand, I saw America as something full of love and light, the sixties music of Redondo Beach in California, Neil Young, Bob Dylan and everything. I had my guitar and a five-octave range, so I knew my musical

"When people hide their light, it can be described as putting your heart away into the willow tree. But you have to shake yourself out of it and not have anything to do with life's limitations."

> "Rouken Glen Park stopped me being
> cynical . . . My past is my past.
> But what it gave me was a ticket to
> learning how to enjoy the now."

abilities could take me around the world, and I decided to share them there.

I loved the way I made people feel when I sang a song. It could be among three old people cooking in the kitchen, or it could be in front of hundreds of people on a street, in a pub, whatever. The feeling that happens between a singer and an audience when they connect, it's the kind of thing that makes the planet go round. I did of course meet people who were cynical about it, but I maintained my Snow White philosophy.

A realist would look at how we were brought up and see deprivation or violence. That was all there. But at the same time, the beautiful thing about human beings is that we can choose how we look at something. Rouken Glen Park stopped me being cynical and middle-aged before my time. My past is my past. But what it gave me was a ticket to learning how to enjoy the now.

You've only got right now, so get on with looking out the window at the beautiful birds trying to survive this rain. I wished for the future I wanted, and a lot of it came true. So now I go back to Rouken Glen Park and I throw money in the fountain, just to say thank you.

RICHARD SCOTT

DUKE OF BUCCLEUCH

NORTH EILDON HILL

RICHARD SCOTT is the 10th Duke of Buccleuch, 12th Duke of Queensberry and Chief of Clan Scott. He was president of the National Trust for Scotland for ten years and is a Fellow of the Royal Society of Edinburgh. One of Scotland's largest landowners, throughout his life he has worked to promote sustainability, rural culture and heritage in all its diversity. He was appointed a Knight of the Thistle by Queen Elizabeth II in 2017.

North Eildon Hill is a really, really important place for me. I feel bound to this hillside at the heart of where my ancestors lived and fought and died, and where the history of the Borders has played out in the surrounding landscape in ways that have always powerfully stimulated my imagination.

From the summit, your eye is drawn immediately to the other two conical points of the Eildon Hills, which together with this hillside are iconic sentinels in the landscape. The horizon scans south past the large column which stands on Peniel Heugh: a monument to the Battle of Waterloo in 1815 beyond the Cheviot Hills and Carter Bar. Then there are all sorts of interesting hills like Rubers Law, with its ancient fort sitting on top, and the Lam-

mermuirs. Directly below, you have the stunning ruins of Melrose Abbey and the site of Trimontium, which was the huge Roman settlement here in the first century AD. Overlaid with that is Old Melrose, where there was a monastery in which St Cuthbert trained before he moved to Holy Island. Then nineteenth-century industrialisation moved into the landscape with a breathtakingly beautiful railway viaduct.

I remember looking out of the windows of our house to check the journey of the sleeper train from London. It had a steam engine and the passage was marked by the train going underneath one of the bridges between here and further south. All of a sudden, the snake would disappear and then back it came. My father, who was a Member of Parliament, often travelled on

> "The power of the place exerts an extraordinary power over my imagination."

the train, and at the end of the week, it was a great childhood pleasure to watch his progress along the last little bit of his way home.

My parents would tell us stories of the ancient Britons, who lived up here on the hill, and the Romans down below. We children used to think of the Romans as wretched, freezing Italians who'd come all the way from sunnier climes. We felt sorry for them, and for the monks trying to carve out a very basic life by the River Tweed, which flows below and in a sense links the whole of the Borders, and we wondered how on earth they survived.

When we were children, the Eildon Hills were virtually our back garden. Living in a house on the side of the hills with dogs and ponies, there was nothing better than to come up here and explore and ride. There was a wonderful slope on the western Eildon which you could gallop your little pony up, confident that it would run out of puff before it got to the top and prevent the danger of you both going over the other side. We'd play all sorts of games hiding on these hills. Because

everything is enormous when you're a child, the highest hill, middle Eildon, with its trigonometrical point at the summit, felt like the very top of the world.

Nowadays, I realise these hills are not the great mountains of the Highlands, and in some ways are quite modest, although they do make a big impression in this landscape. In fact, almost wherever you go, even if you're looking back from Berwick, they act as extraordinarily powerful landmarks that pull you towards them. In any case, the essence of the hills doesn't change. They're wrapped in all these wonderful stories and histories of generations, and they all come together in my head as a long-running narrative that's completely attached to this place. The power the hills exert over my imagination is extraordinary.

As you grow older, you explore and read and learn more. Alongside my own family history and memories, I became quite curious as to how the inhabitants of these hills advanced over the thirteenth, four-teenth and fifteenth centuries. In the days when there was much more woodland, the hills were landmarks. You couldn't see

very far ahead of you, so you needed high points to get your bearings. The lookouts on top of these hills could also warn of the approach of enemies by lighting beacons. For those people, the high points were important and practical.

It's a very rich overlay of millenia of different cultures. If the early assumptions about the Iron Age settlement and the native people on the flank of this hill are true, there were Bronze Age settlers about three and a half thousand years ago. Their almost three-hundred hut floors make it the largest settlement known Scotland. So you've got Iron Age, Roman and Christian people all tangled up in this same small area. I doubt they had the sort of romantic vision that I have of them, living in the twenty-first century with all the comforts that we have, but I still think they were very conscious of landscape here, as were many that came later.

We're really lucky in the Borders with an abundance of great storytellers and poets inspired by the land. You have a wonderful rich mythology of characters like Michael Scott the wizard, who's said by some to have created these hills in the Middle Ages. You have Thomas the Rhymer, who was spirited away by the beautiful elfin queen. If you read Walter Scott's first, great narrative poem, *The Lay of the Last Minstrel*, you'll find that standing on top of this hill, you can trace the rides of the hero from Branksome Tower to Melrose Abbey. The words are

"I see myself almost like a hefted sheep, bound to this hillside."

wonderfully evocative, and those places are all still there. So there's a sort of visual map all around them.

Walter Scott's great house at Abbotsford is just below us, heading towards Galashiels. Over on the hill beyond the viaduct is a famous viewpoint called Scott's View, which was the author's own favourite. When he died and was being taken to Dryburgh Abbey to be buried, it's said that the horses drawing the coffin stopped instinctively at the viewpoint, because they always had.

Walter Scott was an incredibly knowledgeable historian, a passionate antiquarian explorer and gatherer of the storytelling of the Borders. *Minstrelsy of the Scottish Border* was his first great work. For him, this place was the raw material which his vivid imagination turned into both extraordinary poems and his amazing series of Waverley Novels – and he had it all in this small corner of the Scottish Borders. There are others as well, of course, like Scott's contemporary James Hogg, and wonderful poets like Walter Elliot nowadays, the fresh minstrels of the Borders.

So we're in the landscape of poetry and words and abundant tradition, and I'm making it sound very beautiful. But this is also the bloody landscape of the Border reivers. My ancestors were the Border reivers, who tend to be romanticised nowadays, but life was pretty brutal for them. They were the people on the frontline who acted as a defence, keeping the English out and suffering when Henry VIII came in. I think from that history you get a sense of the importance of geography and landscape. They were part of a wild brigand lifestyle, but they were also, in theory, part of the law and order of this way of life, before the English and the Scottish thrones reunited. It all changed in 1603 when James VI became James VI and I of England and abolished Border law. They had to adapt and become respectable citizens, so they did just that.

This journey of my ancestors has always fascinated me. Even now, as I grow older and I'm lucky enough to live in different parts of the UK during the year, I find myself drawn back to these hills. Not just for the pleasure of the views but for the many memories of people who are precious and important to me. My parents and grandparents are buried down below in the wonderful ruins of Melrose Abbey. So there's a feeling of time passing too. I see myself almost like a hefted sheep, bound to this hillside and without the need for a shepherd, as I will always know the place to return to.

KIERON ACHARA

BASKETBALL COURT, CRAWFORD HALL

––––––––––––––––

KIERON ACHARA was the youngest person to play basketball for the Scotland national team. He has made over a hundred international appearances as a professional basketball player and in 2012 he played on the GB basketball team in the London Olympics. After retiring professionally, Kieron has become a public speaker involved in multiple charities and fundraisers. This includes working on the board of OneRen and with children's charity Seamab to improve access to leisure and sporting opportunities for young people. In 2022 he received an MBE for services to community sport.

My perfect place is a basketball court in Stirling I used to visit. I grew up on a nice estate with my mum and brother and had a really good childhood, but I was always different. I was this awkwardly tall black kid in a predominantly white Scottish neighbourhood and I just wanted to fit in.

I started my journey into basketball at fourteen or fifteen, after feeling like an outsider for a long time. I loved sport because I was able to take part and be around people. I had a feeling of acceptance, knowing I could be good at something. Our local park had a long path with a bin at the end of it. It was at my knee height, but the top was very much like a basketball hoop. So I would shoot, shoot, and I got really accurate. Within about two years I went from a kid playing with a basketball to a potential athlete flying over to a camp in America.

When I was there, this coach put his arm around me and said, "Son, if you work really hard, you can get a scholarship." I went, "What's a scholarship?"

He told me, and I soon realised there was a chance I could go to university for free. My main goal initially wasn't to be a basketball player; it was to get a degree, and that was down to my upbringing.

My mum has always been an incredible cheerleader. She helped me embrace who I am and achieve my dreams. She instilled in me that if I was in the right environment, anything was possible. A lot of people's self-belief is completely knocked out of them at a young age, but I was taught I could always adapt and improve. I relished being in environments where I wasn't the best. I think the hardest thing

can sometimes be wanting to challenge yourself, so I'm grateful to feel that guidance in my life. Between Mum and my older brother, I always had support and could channel my energy and motivation into whatever I wanted to do.

Before I left to study, I tended to focus on what I could do to be the same as everyone else. You wear the same shoes, want to look the same, fit into the same box. In my mind, I felt like getting an education was a challenge that would lead to acceptance. I always played it small, never wanted to stand out. I didn't see my differences, which were actually my unique selling points.

Then I went to the States and ninety per cent of my team were black. There was a mixed set of emotions as I had only known an all-white environment. I was learning so much in this diverse place, about myself and the times I hadn't felt comfortable growing up. I was uneasy in this new environment, but there was so much to bring home.

I had embraced my differences and it aligned with who I am, especially from a physical perspective. If I had tried to be a jockey, it might not have worked out so well. Although purpose can be a "do what you love and love what you do" type thing, it's interesting that I didn't love basketball until I found basketball. Then I was good at basketball, so I loved it more.

One year I was back and this court was built. I saw it and thought, *Great!* I'd gone from shooting into a bin to being able to practise all summer on a court. The court was basic, but it could fulfill my needs. I was just grateful to have a flat concrete surface and two hoops to practise with. It felt like it was built for me. It was four minutes' walk from my house and I would be there every day during summer breaks. Whatever was happening, I could go to that court by myself – that was my safe space, my safe haven.

Being home, I also started to see things from a different angle. I had a scholarship to a private university and all the kids there talked about investments and things like that. Whereas at home, everyone just couldn't wait to leave school. So my sense of the world was totally evolving – I was thinking, *If we had some of this stuff where I grew up, a lot of people would want more.*

At that point, my main focus was to get out of the town I grew up in and play for more money. My motivation was based on buying a nice house, having a good car. Once I got my degree, my confidence had started growing. Then people talked about going professional, so that was the next step. I played professionally for a league in Bulgaria and I was getting good money, but I didn't enjoy it. I didn't feel the same level of competitiveness. It was only a job now, which I quickly realised wasn't enough, and that caused me to question my whole career.

I started to think about why I played basketball and my purpose in the sport. Society is always telling us to have more,

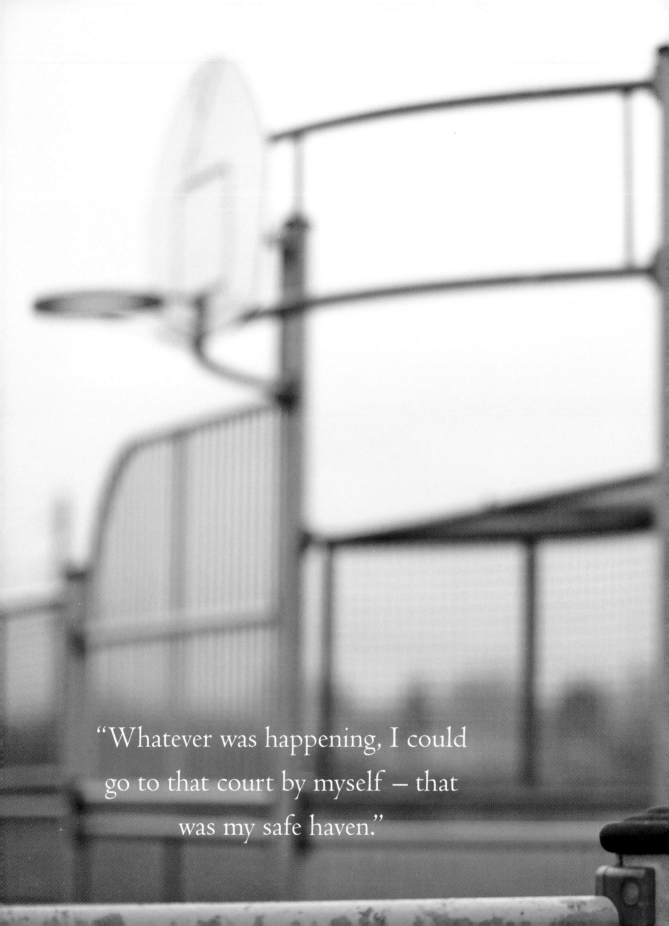

"Whatever was happening, I could go to that court by myself – that was my safe haven."

but I had to step back and question whether that aligned with what I wanted to achieve. Because if it was just for money, I could have another job. So I made the conscious effort to come home to Scotland and play basketball for less money because I knew I could then make a difference in other ways. That led to so many amazing things I could never have expected, including becoming an Olympian.

I know there's so many young people now, feeling how I did when I was looking for my purpose. I think exploring a lot of different things and finding what you enjoy is key. I love basketball and I don't know where I would be without it, but I can't let it define who I am. You can let purpose happen by being experimental, because you may not be doing the same thing you're doing now in twenty years' time. It's more important to build foundations, the ability to work hard, question, critique and find confidence.

Sport is a great tool to help inspire the journey. But people are more than a job title. It's about building inner confidence and not being defined by one thing. You can be super wealthy, with the best job, but it's more valuable having meaning in your life. And I genuinely believe the best way to find that is by helping others.

Being a basketball player, that was a safe space. Now I'm on civvy street and a sporting title will only get me so far. It's overwhelming at times, and sometimes I want to go back to my default because it's safe. But if I'm trying to pursue things, I have to put my feet forward and embrace learning. My ultimate goal is to get into that charity space and make a dent, not as the basketball guy who high fives but as someone who inspires, using focused education and the proper delivery.

I went from the tall, awkward black kid who didn't have a sense of what I wanted to do to someone who people want to utilise as an example for a younger generation. I see people in every industry, and the ones who have the biggest sense of self-worth are the people who are helping others on that journey. I'm inspired by that, and I understand the privilege I have in this position.

I might now be considered one of the lucky ones, but I'm still Kieron from around the way. I come back to this place and look at my situation: how much confidence I gained from playing basketball. Having this space on the court as a sanctuary, where I could just be me, was integral to getting my headspace right and being able to say to myself, *Right, let's go tackle the world.*

For some it's a basketball court; for others it's a library, a youth club or a bedroom. But having a space where you belong and can be yourself is everything. It allows you to build yourself up to be the best version of yourself, so you can give back to others. Being here and playing basketball gave me a sense of responsibility, and with that came a sense of self-worth and self-belief. But most of all, it gave me a place in the universe.

JUDY MURRAY
FISHING LODGE, CROMLIX HOTEL

JUDY MURRAY is a professional tennis coach and mother to two tennis legends – Jamie and Andy Murray, who have 10 Grand Slam titles between them. In 2011 Judy became the captain of the British women's team and since then, she has done much to encourage women and girls to get involved in playing and coaching tennis across the UK. Judy is an advocate for the sport to be more accessible and affordable across Scotland, especially in rural and disadvantaged areas. She was awarded an OBE in 2017 for her services to tennis, women in sport and charity.

My place is a small spot in the woodland around Cromlix Hotel in Perthshire, where you hardly ever see anyone. I would normally come here if I've had a particularly busy time with work or travel, and I'm tired and just don't want to be bothered by anybody or anything.

It's not very far from the hotel, so I park the car and take the walk through the woodland, which is very undisturbed and natural. Muddy too, because we have so much rain up here. I get the wellies on, and the big jacket, and collect my mum and dad's dog. There are lots of great smells for her around here, and she'll run around like mad until we find my little secret fishing lodge, where we'll settle in for a few hours.

If the weather is good, I can sit outside in the sun. If it's miserable, I make my nook

inside the little summer house, because there are a couple of chairs and a little table. I'll never bring a flask because those are for old ladies and I'm not accepting that role yet!

Being near water is always calming and relaxing. The way the world has become, we're all so easily connected to things that I think it's important to give yourself the opportunity to switch your mind off. I'll leave the phone in the car, so I don't get tempted to check my emails or a message.

For the most part, I'll immerse myself in a book. It will almost always be the type of book that I like to read when I'm on holiday: an easy romance or a psychological thriller – books that are incredibly simple to read or books that will make

> *"The way the world has become, we're all so easily connected to things that I think it's important to give yourself the opportunity to switch your mind off."*

sure I'm not thinking about anything else. This one I'm just about to start was written by Carol Kirkwood and it's set on the Riviera, which is the perfect escapism. I might be sitting here absolutely freezing cold, but I can just take myself off to the south coast of France.

I've been writing a novel myself, which is set in the tennis world. So sometimes I'll bring pen and paper to jot down ideas that pop into my mind. Coming here means I can just sit and think about characters or plot lines without interruption. It's an opportunity to weave in a lot of the things I saw and heard and experienced in my career.

The only company you might have are birds – a heron, the odd moorhen or a couple of swans. If the cygnets have hatched, you see their little brood gliding across the water. Otherwise, it's just peace and tranquillity and a whole lot of green.

One of the things I think is just so beautiful about the hotel in general is that you do feel you're in the middle of nowhere. Yet you're only a couple of miles from the M9. When I was growing up, this was always the special place in Dunblane that you went to if you had an occasion to celebrate. My nieces were christened in the small chapel, Jamie was married here, and my mum and dad had their silver and gold wedding anniversaries here. I never would have imagined that one day it would belong to our family.

When Andy decided he wanted to buy it, I tried my best to put him off. I said, "People don't live in houses that big any more." He went, "Oh no, I'm not going to live in it. We can run it as a hotel." It wasn't fit for purpose and nobody wanted to rent it any longer, so I replied, "We don't know anything about running a hotel." He said, "I know, Mum, but you could find out."

So I came up and had a look, and I was really quite shocked that up to six months previously it had been operating as a hotel, given how antiquated the laundry and the kitchen in particular were. There was even

a bat flying around in the billiard room! I remember going back to him and saying, "No, absolutely not. You don't want to buy that. It's falling to bits." As much as I loved the place, it was so old, and it was also a listed building, so taking anything out was going to be full of challenges. But I was also aware that there were lots of hidden gems here too.

That trip was the first time I saw this little fisherman's lodge, which I'd never known of before. I also found a huge shed that stored farming machinery, because a lot of the land around the estate is rented out to farmers. The estate manager showed me inside what I can only describe as a dilapidated metal box. And I went, "Wow, it's huge!" I told the manager, "You could get a tennis court in here." And he said, "Yeah, it used to be an indoor tennis court."

I didn't say anything, but I couldn't believe my ears. When I was growing up, there was no such thing as an indoor court in Scotland. We would play tennis in the ice and snow, and we'd be clearing the courts to try to play in the winter. There just wasn't the infrastructure, and it was very much a minority sport. Instead, I played tennis in the summer and badminton in the winter.

If you couldn't play all year round, it meant you couldn't work all year round, so nobody ever aspired to be a great tennis player or a tennis coach. But there was

actually an indoor tennis court inside this shed, just up the road, all this time. You could still see some of the lines that were there and obviously hadn't been used for ages. I was thinking, *This was here on my doorstep and I had no idea.*

Even when the boys were very small, there still wasn't an indoor tennis court in Scotland until 1994, when they were about six and seven. The four courts opened at Stirling University, which of course was very close to us, and this probably had a big impact on them being able to become good at tennis. If there hadn't been an indoor facility anywhere near us, they likely would have gone off in a different direction. But now, thankfully, we have a tennis court here at Cromlix.

I think Andy wanted this place because it was in our backyard. He wanted something that could be part of the community, where we could employ local people. And even though it needed a lot of work, it's like anything: if you don't know about something, you find somebody who does. And that was what we did. Now, ten years later, Andy and his wife Kim have taken it under their wing and are putting their own stamp on it. It's undergone a major refurbishment and there are plans to build lodges and tree houses on the grounds where guests can experience living among nature.

Being surrounded by nature – water, trees, greenery, animals, birds – is amazing. But I also love the idea that there's a history

> "The outside is very untouched, and I love that
> feeling of escaping into the wilderness."

behind Cromlix too. The main house was built in the 1890s. You park at the house to walk to the fishing lodge and you realise that this was part of a 500-acre estate that would have been owned by aristocracy. It's got a chapel. There are houses dotted around the grounds that were obviously for the estate workers, and it makes you realise that at one time, people did live in these houses and had access to so much space with very little machinery and noise.

So I like thinking about that too, although I'm glad a lot of the old portraits that were on the walls are no longer there, because I always found them really creepy. Either there were no good-looking people in those days or there were just really bad artists. Every time you went upstairs, you were thinking, *Don't look at me*. So I like that the inside is quirky, cool and colourful now. But the outside is very untouched, and I love that feeling of escaping into the wilderness.

I've always lived in small villages and loved getting out to play sport and exercise in the fresh air. I realise not everybody has the option to do that. Maybe you live in a city or don't have spaces like this to wander around in peace and quiet. Being fortunate enough to share that or create that opportunity for others is a wonderful thing to be able to do. And, of course, this is roaming land. People can walk around. Luckily, my little spot should stay peaceful, because most people just don't know it's there.

ALEXANDER STODDART

WEST END CROSS

ALEXANDER STODDART is one of Scotland's best-known sculptors. A fellow of the Royal Society of Edinburgh, he creates neo-classical statues of famous philosophers, scientists and politicians, best known among which are his depictions of Adam Smith and David Hume on Edinburgh's Royal Mile, Alexander's work is also featured in Glasgow's Merchant City and the Sackler Library in Oxford University. He is the King's Sculptor in Ordinary and his architectural friezes stand in the Queen's Gallery at Buckingham Palace.

My perfect place? The answer is absolutely unequivocal. The spot we're going to is known in Paisley as West End Cross. It's a confluence of the High Street, Sandholes Street, Castle Street and, in a way, Well Street. And it's presided over by two architectural masterpieces, making it one of the most focused architectural treasure points you will find in Scotland.

I arrived in Paisley in 1970 when I was ten. I went from a very small house in Elderslie, five miles west, to a large Victorian villa. I remember waking up the first morning in a gigantic uncarpeted bedroom. Out the back of the house there was a field with cattle grazing on it. At the front were the woods of Castlehead. It was as if I had been transported into a kind of miracle place. Just at the foot of the road there was access to town. On that day, I felt I really had everything.

There's a lot of pretty wretched architecture around Paisley, but Well Street is ideal: a street of workers' houses in solid stone tenements. Although dilapidated, they could be restored. In amongst these buildings in the West End Cross are these two marvellous architectural presences.

The first of these is Thomas Coats Memorial Baptist Church, the biggest non-conformist church built as such in Europe. It's in the Gothic revival style, the masterpiece of the Edinburgh architect Hippolyte Blanc. He built several buildings in Paisley under the patronage of the Coats family.

The other one, which sits just behind the church, is a truly remarkable domed structure. Another great architect designed this building – Charles Wilson, from Glasgow. Superbly academically sound and with a very steady hand, he created a mighty school building with a dome in the Assyrian style: the John Neilson Institution, as it was known. It was to this school that I went as a child. I'd walk around the hill called Castlehead, which once had a wee Roman outpost on it, and cross the road to Castle Street and West End Cross. In the spring it's always blistering with blossom.

My fascination with this area really struck when I was in my early teens and I learned about the poet Robert Tannahill. On Castle Street there's a stone marking the place where he was born. It's inscribed with part of a poem:

Here Nature first wak'd me to rapture and love
And taught me her beauties to sing.

As a boy of twelve, finding that on the wall was very significant. I felt his spirit there.

Tannahill was born in one building on Castle Street and he lived in another just across the block. And in the next one, Queen Street, he worked as a weaver in the attic of his cottage. He roamed the Bonnie Woods of Craigielea, which are now part of the cemetery where he was laid to rest and where I too will be buried.

Tannahill was an extreme localist and his poetry was based on the observation of

a very concentrated area on the cusp of town and country. So his focus was geographically very narrow. But at the West End Cross you can still feel his presence. Some folks have a very wide geographical spread but maybe don't plumb the depths so much. Like Tannahill, I am a person who has sought all his life to go nowhere.

People think that to be a famous artist these days you're never off the plane to California or Australia. But the people I grew up with who did that never really got much work done. Their CVs were really just travel logs. On the other hand, you can be extremely far flung on matters intellectual, ethical, spiritual, philosophical and musical without leaving home. Whilst I have had various excursions to

other parts of Paisley, I've lived here all my life. From the family house I could go to the West End, to a hardware shop there, and buy turpentine and linseed oil and brushes for painting. So it was a marvellous proximity when I was starting out as an artist.

I went to art school in 1976. I thought I'd be surrounded by the most sensitive people, aesthetically. But with one or two notable exceptions, none of the students actually seemed interested in art. Nobody liked the History of Art lessons except me. It was a shock. I found myself spiritually discombobulated. So, although we were seen as sad losers at the time, instead of drinking or partying on university trips, my friend Tom and I went to galleries.

"Like Tannahill, I am a person who has sought all his life to go nowhere."

Now Tom is a very esteemed bookbinder, rebinding very, very valuable documents for the National Library of Scotland. And I've got work all over the world.

There's a Roman idea that everybody's got their own genius. It's your guardian angel. It follows you. You must look after it. I've done this within the shortest, tightest possible geographical footprint, but I've still experienced Athens or Edinburgh three hundred years ago, transcending temporal confinement. I'm very lucky to be able to do this.

One of the reasons I love my studio is because it's within hopping distance of the place I've chosen. It's an equally short distance to my house and my grave. The studio is different to West End Cross: it's peaceful. The world here in the studio is quite different from the modern world. It's a very calm place. We're involved in a quietist operation here. Quietism is the calm acceptance of things as they are. And what does a statue do? Precisely nothing all day.

The sight of sculpture looming above us makes us feel tiny. The statues are ignoring us. In other words, they make us feel as though we have ceased to exist. And that is the nature of aesthetic experience. Everything's gone: all your ambitions, all your preoccupations, financial concerns, reputation in the community. Sculpture pours a big pile of water on that ember. It lullabies us. That's what my nature requires: the lullaby as opposed to the fanfare.

I also like to think of making sculpture as something akin to piety. When a statue stands, or sits, in the middle of a street in Edinburgh, that is an embassy of the past. What we're saying with my statue of the great scientist James Clerk Maxwell in George Street, which was unveiled in 2008, is thank you for what you did; thank you for transcending your time on earth by coming up with your four marvellous equations on electromagnetics and giving us, in effect, the modern world. The past is the great reservoir of life.

I would love to see more of my work here in my hometown. I would exchange everything for an exclusive concentration of work in this town. However, the lack of it hasn't caused me to flee or go into exile. I'm still staying for the duration, surrounded by the things I've always looked at.

When I do travel, I'm always very pleased to be home again. I know I'm home when I come through the town in a taxi, hearing the people in the bars and the chip shop, smelling the chips and the petrol fumes, basking in the soft evening in the West End Cross. It's the most modest spot in the world, but it always enchants me.

ROZA SALIH

BELLAHOUSTON PARK

ROZA SALIH is a politician and leading human rights activist. She was born in Southern Kurdistan and her family sought asylum in Scotland in 2001. She co-founded the protest group Glasgow Girls when a fellow student at Drumchapel High School was taken in a dawn raid by immigration officers, a story which has been turned into two documentaries and a musical. In 2022 Roza became the first refugee councillor when she was elected to Glasgow City Council, winning the Greater Pollok ward for the SNP.

My perfect place is on a little hill in Bellahouston Park, overlooking the city of Glasgow. Other parts of the park are popular, but this is my secret place. I think the first time I came here was over six years ago. It feels so natural and peaceful here. There are lovely trees which frame the path and have all these different natural colours, and it's very quiet. You can hear the birds and see the park and Glasgow in the distance.

When my family arrived from Iraq in 2001, we lived in the north-west of Glasgow, but I've been living here in the southside for the last seven years. I moved from north to south to work for the local MP. We have more than sixty thousand people living here. From my little spot I can see Pollok, the area I represent, and I love to see this world, this tiny world, one of the eighty-five council

seats in Glasgow. I've had different jobs in the past, but for someone who came to this city as an asylum seeker, being a councillor has been my favourite.

I wanted a place where I could stop everything, because sometimes it can be so busy with people needing things that I don't even have time for lunch. Other people tell me I need to slow down or I'm going to burn out, so I found this quiet spot in Bellahouston Park, which is huge, to get away from it all. It's about fifteen minutes away from work, so I come here to take peaceful moments and reflect on the world.

As the first asylum seeker to become a councillor, it's quite a lot of responsibility. When you're trying to improve the lives of other people, you can't really say no to anything. You are in a privileged position and feel the need to do something to help. People will ask me to help them translate for their immigration applications and I've worked as a translator before, so I'm like, "Okay, let's do this." It makes me happy that I have accomplished what I wanted as an asylum seeker in this city, and I want to share that.

The Glasgow Girls campaign is what motivated me to speak for people who don't have a voice: minorities and people seeking sanctuary like I did. That was in 2005, and I think that's very important for a young person, having a hope for the future. We were Drumchapel High schoolgirls campaigning to stop the UK Border Agency detaining and deporting children. I've always had that confidence to speak up, ever since I was a child.

My family were very political back home. They stood up to the Saddam Hussein regime, and my grandfather and other uncles were killed by the regime; my uncle was in Abu Ghraib prison for fifteen years. So my family has a long history of fighting for freedom and democracy, and that was something that I recognised as a young person.

I used to ask a lot of questions when I was very young: why we came here, why we left our home. We came from Iraq – we're Kurdish originally – so we went to Turkey. We crossed the borders, walking with donkeys and horses, and we paid smugglers to get us passports. My parents must have been scared. My sister was literally a baby, but I was eleven so it was hard to

know what was happening. But we got on a plane and that's how we came to the UK. We were fortunate because my mum was an accountant and my dad a mathematician. We were middle-class people who had money to do that and probably the ability to work the system. Working-class people would have to take the boat.

I wanted to get an understanding of why this was happening and why we had to leave our home. I didn't really get what was going on and it felt as if my parents had made the wrong decision coming here. The twin towers of the World Trade Center collapsed in the 9/11 attack that year – and we had come to live on the twenty-second block of a high-rise building. I didn't want to be here. We used to have a beautiful house with a huge park for a garden with pomegranate trees, vine leaves and a community around us.

So it was hard. But I understand now why they made that sacrifice. They were scared for their lives, and for our lives. My dad had to bury his family members. People were being killed in the street. So we felt so lucky to be able to come here and have democracy, freedom and basic rights. I still feel so fortunate. My parents instilled in me the importance of those rights, because when they are gone, they are gone.

So I think all of that has made me into a strong person with a hope for a bright future, where people are treated as human beings. It made me want to give back. It gave me confidence in my abilities.

"I come here to take peaceful moments
and reflect on the world."

"I think of so many others who weren't as lucky as
I have been, and I want to change that."

My parents were very vocal in their belief that women should have the same rights as men. My mum worked for women's rights, and she believed that a woman's place was the same as a man's, wherever that may be, in the workplace or the home. She would talk about the people she was helping and raised me to see people as equal. When I see stories of people being mistreated, I think of so many others who weren't as lucky as I have been, and I want to change that.

I'm just so happy that the people in Glasgow have believed in me enough to elect me to this position. And sometimes I do feel the need to do extra work to show I'm capable. If I'm going to a meeting, I want to be extra prepared. I've read all the paperwork, I've made my notes, I'm ready. I always have that need to do extra work, but I think I'm more than capable. When I'm among other politicians and other councillors, I think of what my mum taught me and I say to myself, *I can do this job, okay?*

During my time in the job, I have learned that we all need each other. We need to support our economy and help pensioners, help people who are here in this country to work. There are so many asylum seekers who are not given the right to work and then they get exploited by dodgy employers anyway. These are issues that we need to tackle.

At the moment, I focus mainly on transport, but whether it's housing, health, immigration, benefits, local government issues, young people, education or anything else, I always want to help solve people's problems. But I do of course get a lot of calls which take my time and aren't as important: about someone's cat being stolen maybe, or kids smoking in the garden. So to escape all of that I head to my little oasis only a few minutes away.

I usually bring a blanket and, if it's sunny, I relax with the quiet. I'm reminded of how wonderful the city is. The birds are singing and we have trees and greenery. We have community and we have freedom. Whatever you want to do, it's your life. For me, that's heaven.

JOHN COLQUHOUN

EAST BEACH, NORTH BERWICK

JOHN COLQUHOUN was a star striker for football teams such as Hearts, Celtic, Sunderland and Stirling Albion, scoring over 110 goals and winning two international caps for Scotland. After retiring from football, he was elected Lord Rector of the University of Edinburgh and was a columnist for *Scotland on Sunday*. John is now a successful football consultant and an owner and investor in various businesses he is passionate about.

It's only in the last five or six years that I found my perfect place: a swim in the sea at North Berwick's East Beach. The first time I got into the water, we were walking along the other beach, and I said, "I'm just going to do it." I'd been threatening it for ages and I just took the plunge.

I prefer East Beach to West Beach. It might just be laziness because it's close to my house, or it might be familiarity. Knowing where the rocks are means I won't slip. I know I can swim straight out, because I can see a particular house with a door that I can head towards. It's also a little bit quieter.

I fell in love with North Berwick and East Lothian when I played for Hearts. We used to come up here and stay at the Marine Hotel for European games and big matches. I met a really good friend of mine, the late Pilmar Smith, who was

vice- chairman of Hearts and instrumental in the team coming to North Berwick to prepare for these games. He was an amazing man who educated me about the magic of North Berwick and was dubbed the unofficial Mayor. Those games were some of the greatest nights of my life.

So without being a pseudo-psychologist or a wannabe Freudian acolyte, there will be some connection from that. Being in this beautiful place in the world, feeling those joyous moments when we played against Bayern Munich, when we played against Atlético Madrid, when we played all the big games. There will be some connection, some way that I associate those feelings, moments and occasions with North Berwick.

There are times when I was a footballer that I would have been giving it the Liam Gallagher walk along this beach, but when you get to sixty, you tend not to want that many people to see you in your swimmers going for a dip. When I started, I'd wear a three-quarter wetsuit, but I haven't needed it for about three years now. Once you get into the water and get over that initial, *Ohhh*, there's a feeling of calm.

I'll go in for a morning dip or take a paddleboard and explore. People say, "Oh, you must be freezing when you come out." No! It's cold when you go in, but once you stand for a couple of minutes and do your breathing, you get used to it. When you come out, you're never cold. And there's a serenity that doesn't visit many other times in the day, week or month of the year.

The only way I can describe it is by remembering a commercial on television for Ready Brek, a breakfast cereal. They used to advertise with the slogan "Send You to School". After eating his Ready Brek, the schoolboy would go off with this glow around him and he was heated for the day. That warm glow describes the effect of my swim perfectly. And then of course when you come home, you get into the shower or the bath, which just accentuates it. I'll go into the sea at five or six in the morning, and it sets me up for the day.

When I get out of the water, I'll put my top on and sit on a rock with my coffee. I look out and try to clean my mind and think of just nice things, good things. I try not to think about what I've got to do during the day. Life is so busy and difficult now for the vast majority of

people, and I'm no different. All this stuff going on with different businesses, family, grandchildren: they all add to the busyness and an active mind. You look for something, even just for five minutes, that releases those endorphins and gives you a little bit of peace and tranquillity. I look out over to the Kingdom of Fife and it doesn't matter if it's windy or beautiful or cold and crisp. There's five minutes when nobody can touch you.

I think when you get older, because you've experienced so much joy, sorrow and trauma, sometimes you're looking for something that just settles you. It's a little bit like the feeling of being a footballer. When you go out on the pitch, there are all these pressures: the nerves and anxiety of anticipating the game, all the questions

from the media, manager and coaches. But once you cross the white line, you're on fire. There have been a few times when I've been on fire and nothing – no problems could get in the way. For ninety minutes you were so focused on performing that the roar of the crowd, the buzz and the noise would just keep you going.

There were probably ten times in my career when I had those perfect moments. It's an escape from life, and a lot of players try to find it again through alcohol, drugs or gambling. Once you've had that feeling, you look to recreate it. And there's really nothing else that can.

The competitiveness is also something that's hard to let go. As a footballer, you can play well any day, but when you get

"There's a serenity that doesn't visit many other times in the day, week or month of the year."

> "Being in the water at North Berwick
> settles all those inner pressures."

the big event, the "game of consequence", as it's called, against Rangers, Celtic or Hearts, or a European game, can you do it then? You hold on to that all your life. You don't just say, "I'm hanging my boots up and next to them I'll put my competitiveness." It's in your DNA – you've owned it and used it for seventeen years. You can't just check that in as you walk out of the dressing room for the last time.

It's one of the reasons I play golf. It doesn't matter if you're playing against a nine, ten, eleven or twelve handicap or a scratch golfer, when you've got a four or five foot putt to win the match, the pressure is immense. It doesn't bother me when I've finished playing, but when I'm over that putt, I want to hole it for my team. That's the pressure you put on yourself.

Being in the water at North Berwick settles all those inner pressures. When I'm coming out of the water and I've got five minutes and my week is going well or I've achieved something . . . that's when you think, *Yeah, this is all right.*

My grandchildren live here too. I think it must be the most amazing place to grow up. You have watersports, golf, the Fringe by the Sea festival, a regatta. So much going on. You get to Edinburgh in thirty-five minutes on the train and you can get a seat too, because on either side it's the first stop. When you get to sixty, these simple things are important.

Having said that, you could have a hundred perfect places. I think it's just a place where you feel comfortable alone and don't always have to be with someone. Just to feel that peace. If I could bottle that feeling of sitting by the water looking over to the Kingdom of Fife and Craigleith island, if I could bottle that, I wouldn't make a fortune. Because I wouldn't sell it.

JANICE KIRKPATRICK

LINDSAYSTON BURN

JANICE KIRKPATRICK is a multi-award-winning designer, activist and co-founding Director of the international design studio, Graven. She is one of the UK's top designers and was awarded an OBE for her work in 2013, followed by a Royal Society of Edinburgh Fellowship in 2022. Janice is also a passionate animal advocate and shared the story of her journey to rescue a much loved and vulnerable horse breed from the brink of extinction in a documentary called *Clydesdale: Saving the Greatest Horse*.

There are lots of places around Scotland that are dear to me and have featured largely throughout my life, but the ones I go to are actually very close to home. They are on our South Ayrshire farm and quite nondescript. Well, they're not nondescript to me; they're special to me. And I particularly like the burn. Its official name is Lindsayston Burn and it sits alongside a field behind the house. It's got these massive boulders, great glacial lumps encrusted with moss and lichen and full of wildlife.

We are so fortunate to live in a place where we can just rummage around our own back door into the places we love, to just sit and think of nothing. Nobody's going to find me there, because it's not a destination – just a place I like. I go to a point right at the very end of the field. It's shaped almost like a dog's ear, with a triangular edge. It widens at that point with a tiny left-hand turn, where it's very sandy on the inner side, and that's where the horses and sheep come right down to drink and sometimes just stand in it.

I climb over the fence and wander down through the field along the edge of the burn. It's fenced off from the rest of the field now, so there are celandines, bluebells, campion, just so many wildflowers growing there. They don't get eaten by anybody. The sheep can't get there; horses can't go there.

I can't hear much when I'm there: the sound of the water tinkling along kills the noise of the modern world. The light filters through the trees and you can see insects hatching. There are fish, the odd otter, a badger latrine where badgers dig holes and do jobbies in them, and always this one little dipper, a tiny bird that dives into the water and walks against the stream to pick up things that are living at the bottom. If you're not human, there's a lot of social activity. It almost feels like a huge room, because there's a big canopy with its huge old sycamores, alder and a selection of different trees round about, so it's got this lovely greenish light. Especially when the leaves are out.

I love the mindlessness of just letting things happen around me, nothing to do with me. I'm completely incidental to everything and I'm meaningless in all of it. I can't get enough of the smell, the sound of the water, the feel of it. I'm always on the lookout for interesting stones that might be shaped like items of food or like

people. Those incredible stones underneath are always moving, so the burn changes shape as well. It's endlessly entertaining to see.

I usually wander down there for, I don't know, twenty or thirty feet and it's got a little stony beach on the inside edge of it, which is full of interesting things. I never meet anyone down there, because it's not a place that people go. When I'm there, it's a bit like being a small, muddy child. I don't think I've changed fundamentally; I'm still able to rummage about.

You have to climb out of the bank on all fours, depending on what it's like, and occasionally I get soaked. I like that. I like the fact it's a real thing, not

manufactured. It just is what it is. I find it really reassuring that with all the destruction that goes on – climate change, the decline of the natural world – there's incredible richness in little pockets. The wildlife will come, given a chance, and will flourish and return. There's a feeling of equilibrium that keeps the heart hopeful. I think it's important to slow down and feel that you're part of something bigger and it's going to be okay – but also important to make sure that I do have a say in what happens in my own tiny little space. That makes me feel very good.

In some ways, it's just a very ordinary Scottish burn, but I'd love to know everything that lives in this postage stamp of a place. I've got a kind of secret project. At some point in my life, I'd like to create a massive spreadsheet that records every single thing we've got growing. You know: flora, fauna, everything. I've been thinking a lot recently about Nan Shepherd. She wrote *The Living Mountain* and described in detail a very small area of mountain close to where she stayed. For her, the journey wasn't going up big, tall, impressive peaks, where people compete. It was very much about having an intimate relationship

"I like the fact that it's an endless story that unfolds and I can't control . . . It's a life where there's no pressure."

with the land and the things that live there at different times.

I don't have a favourite season, but I love to see the burn change through the year. It's lovely in autumn when the leaves are falling. Things start rotting, and I like a bit of deliquescence. And I'm still amazed, even in deepest winter, that you get the most wonderful clear days. Despite the rubbish weather, it can be surprisingly nice because the burn is slightly sunken and hidden. Sometimes it freezes over completely so there's a sheet of ice, which makes all sorts of patterns from the air bubbles freezing in the water below.

We've got a badger set nearby and they turn the horse jobbies upside down (because they're frozen like big pancakes) to get the worms underneath. The animals who live here have loads of tricks in order to eat at different times of year. Sometimes, if the sheep are sleeping on a frozen morning, the horses come and push them over with their noses, so they can get the grass that has thawed out while they've been sleeping.

I detest when the clocks change, because the light goes, and that gives me less time to do anything. It always feels like the pressure of holding your nose and going underwater till you come up again, right about the end of March when the clocks change back. Then, in the sticky beginnings of spring, when you have snow outside one day and sun the next, you start to see the butterbur, a big kind of rhubarb-type plant with great big prehistoric-looking, flowery things.

By summer, the sun rises early, with the thrush singing in the morning. There's so much life emerging from the burn. I find a stone to sit on, or a place to cross to the other side, depending on how high the water is. You can feel that it's alive with things to see, things to smell, things to hear. Others that I can't sense but I know are burrowing about. You think you know everything and then something else turns up that you haven't seen before.

Recently we've had nuthatches, which have moved up from down south. I also keep bees, which are a joy, as my father did. I really love seeing pollen beginning

"The sound of the water tinkling along kills the
noise of the modern world."

to happen. It provides them with protein and allows them to start laying eggs to create new bees for the next season. The bees go into the hive, and because different kinds of pollen are different colours, you can see what the pollen parcels are on the bees' legs. That tells you which tree or which flower they've chosen this time of year. If it's tree pollen that they're taking into the hive, you know they're starting to think about feeding a brood.

My father would have loved the burn. He was an amateur entomologist. There are so many insects, and every time you look, you learn something. I like the fact that it's an endless story that unfolds and I can't control. I can nudge things, but I can't control them. It's a life where there's no pressure. And I think that's a really wonderful thing because everything I do in my professional life as a designer is about control and it's usually within a metropolitan environment.

I've lived here now for twenty-three years and I could never live in a city again. I like being there for part of the week to work, but home is here. I couldn't bear the thought of being removed from nature. You can give yourself permission to make a little fire, sit down, you know, talk to a goose, and there's always somebody who wants scratched. Yes, the radio is still there in the background, telling of the horrors happening everywhere. But you can choose to turn it off and listen to the thrush instead.

Quite often, we don't give ourselves permission to do things, because people say, "Oh my God, you travel for an hour and a half!" I mean, people travel that long just to get from one end of London to the other and think nothing of it. I can still connect to wherever I need to connect to, as they also can. And I can just leave the house at the back door – I never get tired of being able to do that.

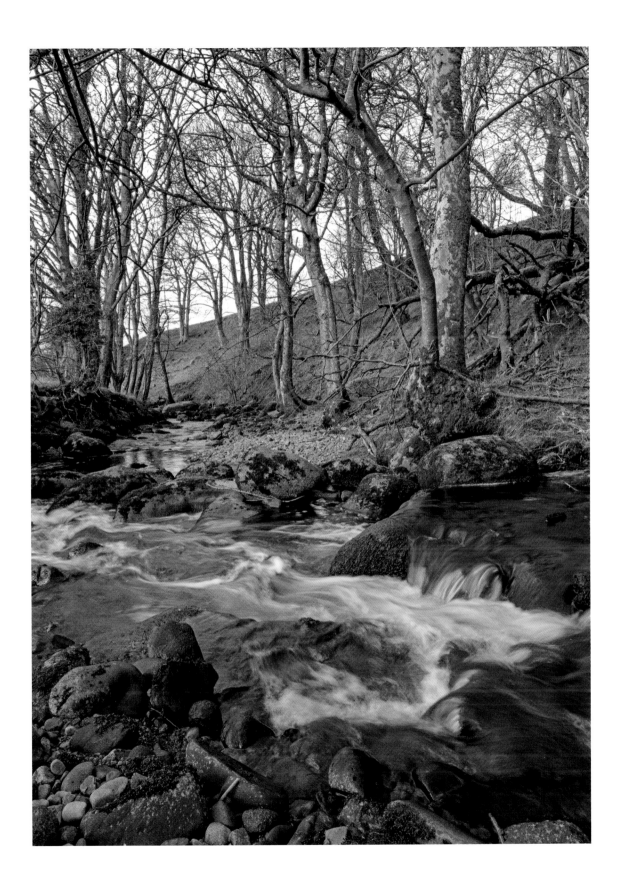

CATRIONA MATTHEW

18TH HOLE, GLENEAGLES

CATRIONA MATTHEW is a professional golfer who grew up in North Berwick. She is a member of the Ladies European Tour and has achieved many victories including the Ricoh Women's British Open in 2009. Catriona frequently competes in the Solheim Cup and was captain of Team Europe when they won the competition at Gleneagles in 2019. She was awarded an OBE in the 2020 New Year Honours for services to golf.

The first time I really fell in love with Gleneagles was in 1998, when I won my first professional golfing event in Scotland on the King's Course. It was the McDonald's WPGA Championship of Europe – possibly the longest title ever; I don't know how they managed to fit it on the trophy. I jumped at the chance to play here and ended up coming out on top, beating Laura Davies, Helen Alfredsson and some of the people I really looked up to and had admired as an amateur.

Ever since that first victory, I've enjoyed coming back. Gleneagles is totally different to what I'm used to. I grew up, and still live in North Berwick by the coast, so the scenery in the glen here, surrounded by hills, is a great contrast. Having said that, growing up in North Berwick is probably what started me playing golf. There are so many courses there, and my mum and dad played, as well as my older brothers.

My parents never pushed me, but they were always really supportive. I think if you want to be good at anything, you can't have someone standing over you saying, "You've got to go and practise." You've got to want to do it yourself. I was the one tagging along with my brothers and probably annoying and pestering them, but I think that pushed me to keep up. I was a typical sporty tomboy of a girl, and I was very lucky I had the opportunity to try lots of different things and find the one I had the passion for.

I remember my mum would take me to golf tournaments, and eventually, when I was sixteen or seventeen, I realised that was the sport I was best at. I wanted to focus on golf as a career, so I went for it. I got into the Scottish team and managed to get a scholarship for university. I studied accounting and during that time decided I definitely wanted to turn pro. I

"When I'm playing the King's or the Centenary course at Gleneagles, it's amazing how you remember — even all the way back to the nineties — the shots you hit or where you went."

feel really fortunate to have played well and stayed on for the next twenty-five years, as any sport at the top level is cut-throat and pretty tough, so not many make it.

Luckily it worked out, and my parents loved coming out on tour to different places across the world. They got to travel all over, and then, when I met my husband and we started a family, they were fantastic babysitters. I have to give my husband a lot of credit as well, as he was willing to give up his job so he could caddy for me and I could continue to pursue my career, even when the kids were little. Looking back, I have no idea how we did it, but we all travelled the world on tour, and we made so many fun memories.

In an individual sport like golf, you're always looking for improvement, trying to reach that top level and never feeling you've quite made it. Then you go out and play against the best in the world and see how you fare against them. It makes it all worthwhile to come out with the trophy. That's what all the hours of practice are for, and there's no better feeling. In golf you won't ever win many, no matter how good you are, so every win feels special.

I had a particularly amazing year in 2019 – and Gleneagles was at the heart of it. First, we came for a European team-building day with the women golfers I was captaining for the Solheim Cup, a tournament held every two years between Europe and the United States. That was a fun day.

We were driving around blindfolded to bond the team. And it obviously worked, because we won the cup that year!

It's totally different winning in Scotland in front of your home crowd, as we did at Gleneagles that September. At one point, it looked as if we weren't going to win, and then three matches just went our way. I was coming up to the last hole. It had all come down to the final match and then the sun came bursting out. In the end, it came down to Suzann Pettersen, who holed a five-footer putt to clinch it for us all. I remember running on to the green to congratulate Suzann and then, what felt like ten seconds later, the whole crowd kind of enveloped us on the green. It was just an incredible experience, which felt like a culmination of my whole career really. For that to happen, and to be a captain, and to do it in Scotland felt so momentous. It's lovely coming back to Gleneagles to relive those memories and make more.

It made it even more special that my daughters raised the flag on the stage during the opening ceremony that year, although it did very nearly go wrong. Someone behind me said, "You'd better go and help them." Then there was a magic puff of wind and thankfully all disaster was averted.

I've got a great photo I dug out the other day and my older daughter said, "What did you make me wear!"

I thought they had very good outfits, matching yellow and blue for the European flag, but I'm not sure she's on board quite yet.

Still, that was a great moment for us and their grandparents to watch. To have that as the start of the tournament and then go on to win and have such a perfect end to the weekend is something I'll always cherish.

When I'm playing the King's or the Centenary course at Gleneagles, it's amazing how you remember – even all the way back to the nineties – the shots you hit or where you went. At the Solheim, I've obviously watched a lot of golf, being the captain. You can remember a player being there and the shot they hit. When you're playing, it's great fun because you're at the peak of your career, but there's obviously a lot more pressure and you want to go out and play well. If you don't play well, you feel as if you've let your teammates, your captain, your country, your continent down. So when you're playing, you're so focused on having to hit the shot that you don't really see anything but the ball.

When you aren't playing though, you can look around and be more aware of your surroundings. Even though there are thousands of people, you can always pick out a few you know. It's an amazing part of the experience to be able to listen to the crowd singing their songs and cheering and shouting. Whenever I came to par three, there were people I knew standing at that tee, and I loved watching them all playing down there. So now every hole has its own little memory as I play it.

These days, I also come to Gleneagles just to relax with my family. They absolutely love coming here. We try to stay once a year, and our favourite things all seem to revolve around eating. We have a good breakfast and we occasionally take them out to play a wee round of golf, although they seem to be more drawn to the pool and the spa. It's amazing how you can while away the time here doing lots of different things. I've tried the fly fishing, which I was absolutely hopeless at, and the shooting, which I did quite well in.

So with all those great golfing experiences and the fun we have in our family breaks, Gleneagles is a very special place for me. I think it's really important to find somewhere that holds happy memories. It can be anywhere, but as long as it holds significance for you, then you always have that memory to revisit.

VICTORIA STAPLETON

BRORA

VICTORIA STAPLETON is the founder and creative director of Brora, a luxury manufacturer of cashmere products. Victoria first came up with the idea of starting a textiles company thirty years ago when her family became involved with Hunters of Brora, a hundred-year-old tweed mill in the Scottish Highlands. Brora prides itself on being a sustainable brand, and all of its cashmere is ethically sourced. It currently has ten boutiques, including two in Edinburgh and one in New York.

I've settled on the village of Brora on the Sutherland coast as my perfect place. The mix of happy memories going back to my twenties and the extraordinary geographical nature of Brora, being all hills and river on the one hand and fabulous beach on the other, makes it pretty ideal. Both personally and professionally, it's very special. In fact, I don't know where my life would be if I hadn't gone to Brora when I did, because it's been the starting point of everything I've done since.

Brora is nestled on the east coast about an hour north of Inverness. As you drive through the village, there's a stone bridge taking you over the River Brora, a famous salmon-fishing spot, and up to the station square where the old Hunters of Brora shop used to be. To the disappointment of a few seasoned tweed mill visitors, it's now a curry house.

If you take one of the roads off to the right, you drive up to the waterfront and the mercury waves roll in on to kelp-covered slabs. When the children were small, they would play in the rock pools and we would collect the mussels growing there. My husband is always good at making a fire. He had this little tin can that we'd put seawater in to cook up the mussels and have a picnic.

There is a charming harbour and, of course, the Brora links golf course, a favourite of many who enjoy this frustrating sport! From the first hole you see over all the mountains and in the distance, you get a view completely out to sea. I love the anticipation and excitement of being outside and walking for hours.

I was brought up in Cumbria, but we often came to Scotland for holidays because my grandfather lived just ten miles from the border. His house was very near a river and we were taught to fish by my father, who was fanatical about trout fishing. If we weren't fishing, we were just in our undies stepping across the river, collecting pebbles that we then took home and painted. We were quite hardy as children. We were four sisters and my father made it clear that he wanted a boy, so we all became very boyish, very quickly.

Brora became part of my life when my family bought the old tweed mill in the village. The mill was started by a Mr T. M. Hunter in 1901 and had been a big employer in the village for many decades. In the late eighties, when so much manufacturing moved abroad chasing higher margins, Hunters of Brora was one of the casualties. My father had an emotional attachment to the cloth produced there, so when he found out that the doors were about to close, he set about trying to rescue the mill. Knowing nothing about the textile trade, he persuaded a few others to join him in relaunching these age-old designs.

At this point, I was asked to revamp the old shop in the centre of the village and create an emporium of the very best Scottish textiles, made both by the mill in Brora and by other renowned Scottish mills. We created a cosy, tartan-carpeted shop full of cashmeres, woollens and tweeds, and it became a destination for those on holiday in the area.

That's where I learned about how tweed was woven and colours were put together; about what you could make with various different patterns, different weights of tweed; about how you could use it in hundreds of ways, depending on what you were going to do with the finished product.

I remember very well the stunning drive from Inverness airport to Brora, knowing every twist and turn in that well-trodden road. I used to stay at the Marine Hotel with views out across the ocean. In summer, when the nights were very long and work was done for the day, I would go for walks on Brora Beach.

When I met my husband, it was really quite extraordinary that he said, "I'd like you to meet my parents. They're going to be fishing on the River Helmsdale." We had this instant connection owing to our love of the Highlands. His memories of Helmsdale up the road were as rich as my memories of Brora.

After a few years, those running the tweed mill decided that they didn't need me to run the shop and product-development side, so my job in Brora came to an end. It was an emotional moment, and for a while I visited Brora less often. But because of my husband's connection with Helmsdale, I always spent some time close by every summer.

Then I decided to start my own retail business, creating the very best Scottish

"Whether I'm away from it or near,
I take this place with me, because I'm
always working with those colours
and that inspiration."

textiles. As in any business endeavour, to build the brand, I've had to make loads of mistakes and take loads of risks – but I've learned over the years that I don't get terribly anxious, and mentally I do have some resilience. That's partly because of the way I was brought up. I was thrown into independence very quickly and more or less told to get on with it. I was the third child and my parents were busy working, so I watched my two elder sisters and learned from them. It taught me to get out and do my own thing and always focus on opportunities.

In the course of thirty years, that philosophy has transformed my idea into the fashion brand called Brora, selling head-to-toe looks with a very personal aesthetic and making so many of our designs in the British Isles.

In the village of Brora itself, I see inspiration for my designs everywhere. There's the harbour with the lobster pots and fishing boats, the multi-textured pebbles on the beach, the bright yellow gorse, the heather in summer and the sky and cloud formations. All this mood-boosting colour. If you took the shades from a beach, depending on the time of year, you could come up with many different palettes of lovely washed-out blues and greys and pale yellows. Then in the summer you've got the kelp, which is that really insane bright green, but also seaweed like henna – a dark, orangey

brown colour – and all that mixed in with the shades of the sea. The other day when I was there, the sea was what I would call a mercury colour. It was a grey blue, and if you mix that with the hennas and the kelp colours, that's a really rich autumnal winter knit.

So whether I'm away from it or near, I take this place with me, because I'm always working with those colours and that inspiration and that mood board and that backdrop. And what I learned in the village of Brora in my twenties has been instrumental throughout my entire life. Especially with the next-door village being my husband's perfect place. It's like an extraordinary synergy that has been a shared interest for the last twenty-six years.

Brora really is a part of my soul. For a while it was hard to go back, but now I feel once again the magic of the place. I have lots of happy memories of both my parents and my in-laws, and now we come to play golf and fish for salmon, or as often sleep and read on the riverbanks because the water is too low or too high. It's just a great place to have fun and be at one with the astounding natural beauty.

Here you feel you can trust your environment to take care of you. You feel relaxed and also want to explore. It reaches that part of you in an almost secret way, an inexplicable way that is very special.

GRANT STOTT

BLACKFORD HILL

GRANT STOTT is an award-winning radio and TV presenter, actor and columnist. An established villain at *The Edinburgh Kings Theatre Panto* for twenty-five years, he is a regular at the Edinburgh Fringe and gained critical acclaim for his own one-man show *Tales from Behind the Mic*. Grant's television appearances include *Outlander, Children in Need* and *Scotsport*. He is currently playing the role of Sam Spiller in *River City* alongside hosting a weekly radio show, *Vinyl Collective*, each Friday on BBC Radio Scotland.

I just love walking up Blackford Hill. You pass the old buildings, walk up the grassy knoll, and the whole skyline of Edinburgh stretches out in front of you. It's a total contrast between city and nature, and I think that's what I like so much about it. On a clear day, you can see all the way to Fife and North Berwick.

Over lockdown, we wanted to make a little video that we could send out to the fans of the panto who come every Christmas. I was wondering what to do, so I came up here and looked out over there and decided to read the lyrics to my song "That's Fife" as a poem, strolling along on my daily one-hour walk with Fife in the background.

I chose this part of Edinburgh because it has become such an important place to me over the last twenty-five years. I was thinking of choosing the Bruntsfield

area, because throughout my entire life it has been – and still is – significant. Yet another huge part of my life was moving to this side of town, having a family and discovering this place.

If you ask me if I remember coming up for the first time, well, no. This place has been a forever constant in my life. I probably came up here as a kid. The south-west of Edinburgh is where I grew up, so this whole area is very familiar to me, especially the Braid Hills and Braidburn Valley. My mate, when I was ten or eleven, lived on Mortonhall golf course, so on holidays we would go up there looking for golf balls and get trapped in the gorse bushes.

It ticks all the boxes. A place to escape. A place to go away and stick music in your ears. A place to come when it's snowing. A place to come when it's sunny. And for me, it's a place where we have all grown up as a family.

I used to bring my kids to sledge as soon as we could see the snow come in. We started doing this when they were really wee, which inevitably meant I was back and forth doing heavy lifting. They'd slide all the way down and I'd be painfully pulling the sledges away back up the hill.

When my son was little, I bought him one of those wee planes that fly and we decided to take it up there. He's flying this thing and it's going up and up, and I'm going, "Very gently, very gently. Don't go too close to the edge, because if it goes over, that's it, we've lost it."

He wasn't getting it, so I said, "Look, I'll show you," and *vrrrooom* it goes right over. I could never forget his wee face. I've never felt such a baddie in my life. When the two of us looked over the edge, it was stuck halfway down this quarry.

The next day, with a wee bit of a hangover, I got up some courage and came back. I looked up and there it was. I climbed halfway up the quarry face and managed to grab it, at which point I turned to throw it down and actually looked at the height. Oh no! Absolutely terrifying. But when I got home, there was his wee face, totally delighted.

Both my kids have shown a desire to go and explore somewhere other than Edin-

burgh, which is really bizarre as it's pretty much the opposite of what I wanted to do growing up. I was big into my music, so I'd go to Princes Street, which had record stores all around. Even towards Tollcross and Morningside there were great clothes shops and nightclubs, and places like Coasters, the roller rink where I worked as a DJ. I wanted to get out into my own city and thought I'd lucked out growing up in Edinburgh. I worked a lot in Glasgow in the nineties, so I could have moved through there. Obviously London was a possibility for work too, but I had everything I wanted here.

When I left school, I joined the police, who sent me to Jedburgh. I lived in the Borders for two years, which was a bit of a culture shock for an eighteen-year-old DJ. I was just desperate to get back. I realised I wasn't the most suited to that job so I came home. I joined Radio Forth, and the first thing we did was for an article in the *Evening News*, where they made me bring my police hat and a copy of a single by The Police. That was one of my first publicity shots.

I tried out for drama college but got turned down. That was my first real rejection in life and there were so many times I thought that acting wasn't going to happen. I never gave up though. I think things happen to you for a reason and that includes the bad stuff. If you don't get what you want, then it just wasn't right for you at that time. That doesn't mean it isn't in your future or you should give up.

"That's what I love about Edinburgh. It never takes too long to get out of the hustle and bustle and find a spot like this."

I've had a few examples of that in my life.

I was just starting in television as a presenter in 1993. I was doing children's TV and had enough experience to put together a showreel. I put the VHS in Jiffy bags, with a note saying, "If you're looking for a TV presenter, I'm your man." Then I sent the tapes off to various TV companies.

One of them was STV in Glasgow, who returned the showreel with a letter saying, "Sorry. Nothing on the go, but if anything comes up, we'll keep you in mind." Well, that same day I opened the newspaper only to find a big article inside headlined, "STV Hunt for New Saturday Morning TV Presenter". I was so gutted and furious. Then I thought, *I'll just do it*. I got a new Jiffy bag out and sent the same tape back to STV with the article in mind. Well, I got the audition and I got the job! I'll always remember that moment. If my ego had got in the way and I'd decided I was too good to send the tape back, I never would have got that job, which was a massive turnaround for me – one of my first big breaks in television.

I've had brilliant jobs and I've lost brilliant jobs. New bosses come in, series get axed, shows change – but you can't get hung up on that. In the early part of my career, I learned from experience and from speaking to others that it's not really anything to do with you: it's just circumstance. You might not have the look they want or sound right for that particular job. So you wait until there's a job you are perfect for. And you never give up.

My current role as Sam Spiller in the BBC Scotland soap opera *River City* has been a big life achievement for me. It's something I wanted for a long time. After all the auditions, knockbacks, finding different ways to get into the industry and searching for the roles that were meant for me, thirty years on I get a gig on *River City*!

It's about understanding that you can put your heart and soul into something and they might just ditch it. But then you've got to say, "Okay, what am I doing next?" You move on to something that's going to be a fit for you and, with the support of people around, you try to get to a point where you feel good again. Even when things are bad, you can go somewhere to clear your head. And that's where Blackford Hill comes in. I wander up there, enjoy the skyline, the nature and think of good memories.

Every time I reach the hilltop, I think, *I don't come up here enough*. It's literally a five-minute walk from my house. You're right in the centre of this huge capital city, walking up a hill with a mesmerising view, surrounded by green hills, bushes and fantastic scenery.

That's what I love about Edinburgh. It never takes too long to get out of the hustle and bustle and find a spot like this. I'll leave to travel and visit my kids around the world, but I've never felt the need to up sticks, and I'll never regret staying in this wonderful city. I've managed to achieve everything I wanted, and my family and career have all blossomed while living here in Edinburgh. It's really life-affirming.

KEZIA DUGDALE

LOWER LARGO

KEZIA DUGDALE is a writer, campaigner and former politician. She was leader of the Scottish Labour party for two years and was an MSP for the Lothian region for almost ten years. Kezia is now Director of the John Smith Centre for Public Service at the University of Glasgow, alongside being a board member for charities including Shelter UK and Sistema Scotland. She has a public policy podcast, *Spotlight,* was a contestant on *I'm a Celebrity . . . Get Me Out of Here!* and is also a columnist for *The Times* and *The Courier* amongst other publications.

It was always going to be a beach for me. There's something really cleansing and peaceful about the water that I've associated with peace throughout my whole life. So I've picked Lower Largo in Fife.

Lower Largo is close to where I live now in Markinch. I can come here even when I just have a spare hour, but it's also somewhere we visit as a family during the holidays. We've had some momentous nights, celebrating when my wife was re-elected to the Scottish Parliament, having my fortieth birthday here. It's associated with a lot of really good memories.

At the back of the house we stayed in for my fortieth were steps from the balcony down to the beach, and we were blessed with the most amazing weather. It was

twenty-four degrees. In August. For a whole week. Almost every night we ate outside the Crusoe Hotel under a big canopy. We would watch them bring the fish in from the boat, straight into the restaurant. There aren't many places in Scotland you can still do that, so there's a real authenticity to this place.

Lower Largo is very quiet and not particularly touristy. If you keep going east, you get to Anstruther and Pittenweem and Elie, which are still like old-fashioned fishing towns but with a lot of tourism. It's not the same here. People live their whole lives in Lower Largo, and not many know about the beaches with all their little alcoves. I quite often just come down to my favourite one and sit. I can find peace pretty quickly and easily on that little bit of rock.

You feel the incredible quality of the air running through your system. There's also something quite powerful about the combination of the rock with its many layers, thousands of years old, and the trees which are changing every second. I absolutely love that combination of constant features and new rolling cycles.

I spend lots of time looking out to the sea, but if you turn the other way, you can see Scotland's past in the metal structures past the shore. All of that metal represents how hard this area was hit in the eighties by the decline of the coal industry, shutting down the mines, mills and factories.

Then, further on, you have the beginnings of regeneration. You can see Leven in the skyline. It's getting a railway station for the first time, which will bring so many opportunities to young people living there. Beyond is the renewable base, a new industrial life just beginning. So there's a fantastic future for Scotland to be seen from here as well. It's about recognising the past and welcoming the next part.

I was born in Aberdeen and grew up in Elgin, where my dad's rule was "be home by dark". In the winter we had no time at all; but during those summer nights in the nineties, ten-year-old me was out all hours in the park or near the river after school. My parents were both teachers, and a lot of my values come from them both really believing in education and what it could give people. I left there when my mum got a new job and we moved to Dundee.

I think going to secondary school in Dundee eventually made me into a bit of a city kid, but on my first day I was absolutely astonished by the place. It was a cement building with a cement playground and no grass. And I was like, *What is this?* I couldn't believe it at the time, but I came to understand that there were – and still are – many, many kids who go through their whole childhood without ever experiencing the proper outdoors. That was mind-blowing to me.

From Dundee, I went to Aberdeen to study and then I moved to Edinburgh. I'm firmly an east-coaster, although I never thought I would leave Edinburgh. I was a total city girl by that point and it was Edinburgh that I represented in the Scottish Parliament. I lived ten minutes from work, just to the back of Meadowbank. I felt lucky that I could be at my desk so quickly from home, but I did live in a top-floor flat, which was beautiful but small. I didn't spend anything like the amount of time that I do outdoors now, on the beach or in the garden.

When I lived in that small top floor flat in Edinburgh, I was leader of the Scottish Labour party. My life was politics and I worked up to fourteen-hour days, seven days a week. I loved it. It was hard, but I loved it. I'm very proud of the time I spent as leader, but there were things that happened, and all the difficulties that come with being in the spotlight and being a woman in politics, which were hard to manage alongside living your own life.

"In good times and in bad, I always find
myself being drawn towards the beach,
the rhythm of the sea and the waves."

It was during those latter stages of being party leader that I lost my best friend to motor neurone disease. He was twenty-nine. We had lived in the same building and worked together for a long time. When he died, after surpassing all expectations and living with MND for twenty-eight months, it really made me wake up and ask myself if I was happy. The answer was no. At that point, I had to work out what I could control about my life in order to be happy. Because what is life for if you don't enjoy it?

I started to make big changes and decided to walk away from leadership. I didn't automatically think I was going to leave politics, but an opportunity came to move out of that as well and I took it. I moved into my partner's old house in Markinch and now I'm nearly four or five years out of politics and a lot happier. I work for the University of Glasgow, largely from home, so I spend a lot more time outdoors. I can work hard in a job I love, or on charitable interests, but I still have time to walk the dog and potter around in the garden.

My partner had quite a traditional garden when I moved in. It had been there since she bought the house a couple of years earlier. It was slabbed and had lots of chuckies and pebbles, lots of perennial plants and some bushes, all a bit dull. We knew we wanted to spend more time outside, so we took it upon ourselves to renovate it. Everyone told us we couldn't do it and needed to get help in, but one week in the Easter holidays, we filled five skips and removed forty tonnes of rubble. We lowered the garden

by about two feet and started planting. I loved every minute. It felt awesome.

If you'd told me five or ten years ago that I would be glued to Monty Don and *Gardener's World* on a Friday night, I would have laughed you out of town. But now I'm living this completely different life. I spend most of my days in wellies or at the beach in Lower Largo walking my dog, who would also describe it as his perfect place.

I associate this place with a lot of happy memories and history, but it's also an anchor point. There's something about the tides that teaches you about balance and the importance of everything being in equilibrium. In good times and in bad, I always find myself being drawn towards the beach, the rhythm of the sea and the waves. It hits your brain in all the right places.

When I'm faced with something that I don't know how to resolve, I can take myself to that water, on a wee rock, not being disturbed, just having a think. I always leave with some sort of path or idea through it. I think everybody should find a place like that for themselves. It doesn't have to be a stunning beach or in the woods: it could be right in the centre of the city. As long as it's a place that allows you just to stop.

I've got a new career and a much better work-life balance. My wife is in the forefront politically now and I'm able to support her and hopefully be of some use, given what I've experienced. You will find her in parliament and me in the greenhouse or on the beach.

NATI DREDDD

GLENCOE

NATI DREDDD is a folk singer and social-media star from a seaside town in Fife. She rose to fame sharing covers of famous songs on TikTok and currently has nearly 2 million followers. She has supported acts such as Newton Faulkner, Simply Red and Tidelines, and headlined the River Stage at TRNSMT 2023. She is currently touring Scotland, releasing new music and has appeared as a featured artist on *The Scotsman Sessions* and BBC Radio Scotland.

My perfect place is the lochan in Glencoe. It's a little hidey-hole with mountains and water and lots of trees. The trees were planted by Lord Strathcona in the nineteenth century: apparently he was hoping they would comfort his Canadian wife, who was homesick for trees. I'd found a lot of photographers from that area and I was just enchanted by their images. I have no shame in saying that when I finally went there and saw the mountains and the rain over the water, I burst into tears. That was when I knew this place was another home.

I've always been attracted to nature. That's what pops me back into my body and back into reality. I love getting my hands dirty and my feet in the soil. Even when I was little, I used to be obsessed with landscapes. I was the child climbing trees, falling out of them over and over

again, and getting stuck in the mud on purpose.

As a musician, I'm also inspired by the natural world, whether it's something like the rain peppering the water or the sunset when you're climbing the mountains. Music has always been an important presence in my life. My mum said I sang before I spoke.

There was a period when I almost lost that part of myself – and it was this place that saved me. It was a time when I was working all the hours I could. I had two jobs, one of which I detested. It was very loud and full of technology and beep-beeps. I was constantly looking at screens. I was in a glass box, literally. I was away from light. I felt as if it was fading the colour from me. There would be days when I'd go home and look at my guitar and wouldn't want to pick it up. I wasn't singing in the shower. I wasn't singing on the toilet. That was really upsetting because I've always been able to turn to music. I lost a huge part of myself, and I was in a really, really horrible place. Most days I felt like a little mushroom.

But one day, like a dog, I took myself for some walkies. I went to Glencoe, and I had a moment of just exhaling all of that. And I snapped back. I came home and wrote a song that I now sing on stage called "Apocalypse", which was about my experience of that job. It helped me immensely, just getting out and about.

I think the thing that drew me to Glencoe that day was the silence. There's a gentleman called Kevin Woods, who climbed 282 Munros, all in a hundred days for charity. He said this: "There's a silence that only mountains can give you." I went and felt this intense sensation of being enveloped in comfort and silence, and I was like, *Oh my God, he's right.* Even now, I love doing music, but it's a very loud career, full of people. So going to the lochan and feeling that silence wash over me is like magic.

The first thing I do when I get there is just breathe in. It's the freshest air, the nicest smell. You've got the salt from the sea-loch beyond and the dirt all mingled in, which doesn't sound very sweet-smelling, but it is to me! I take a big deep breath and say out loud, "I'm home!" I love it. Then I casually meander all the way up to the lochan and sit for a minute: just sit in

my bones and take it all in. It's not even a reflective state that I go into. I just enjoy the peace.

I'm a person who likes to do everything, all at once. One of my flaws is that I'm quite impatient. If there's a project that I'm working on, I want it done yesterday. So one of the things I struggle with is mono-tasking. I think we can all be the same. Say you have a cup of coffee or tea in the morning. When was the last time you just sat and drank it without going on your phone, checking your emails, tidying, doing other things? Even at the weekends I think we're quite guilty of it as well. You're catching up with your friends or your family or rushing about. I feel like we could all do ourselves a favour by just drinking that bloody cup.

One of the good things about the Highlands is that there's often no phone reception. Even if people want to reach me, they can't. It's like having your phone on airplane mode. I like going places where you're not gettable. The answer to "Where's Natalie?" is: "Where she wants to be. Leave her alone!" I'll go there to get away from everything and just be with myself in the moment.

Still, one thing does come to mind when I'm up there. I know it sounds cheesy, but it's gratitude. There's something so beautiful about how rugged Scotland is. When you drive through Glencoe, you suddenly notice there are fewer and fewer buildings and more and more fields, and then suddenly these big shadows loom over you, and you're just in awe of their

"Get your hands in the dirt. Get your feet in the soil. Find a place that's just for you."

presence. All these hills and mountains and cliffs and lochs and everything, all chipped and cracked and old, and the waters running through them – they've all got so many stories to share. I don't want something that's small and smooth and pretty and sparkly. I want something that's big and intimidating and rough around the edges. I find beauty in that.

Maybe that's why I feel so present among this bare ruggedness. Being in this kind of environment has an amazing way of grounding you, and it could either mean that you have an epiphany moment and you think, *I know what's wrong*. Or that you finally feel a moment of peace. When you're struggling mentally, you do have to sit with yourself and isolate everything you're feeling and try to figure it out. And not only that, but you have to go through every option. Can you afford some therapy? Do you have anyone you can talk to? Can you go on an online forum and talk to people? Do you have a hobby or something you can do that will fulfil you? And if you go through that and you still feel lost, I think a place is so important. Because sometimes it just feels hard to do any of those things.

If you can walk somewhere and find a little corner of the world that's yours for a minute, that can bring you back to earth; it's a key element of any mental health journey. I would encourage anybody who's feeling that way to start small. If you can't sleep, open the window at four o'clock in the morning and listen to how silent the world is. Slowly but surely make those steps and get outside and go for a walk.

You need that moment because if you've exercised all options and you still can't escape those mental muddy waters, at least you have a little haven, your own safe space. Get your hands in the dirt. Get your feet in the soil. Find a place that's just for you or maybe just you and a trusted friend or a loved one. A change of scenery.

For me it's going to that rugged wilderness. It switches everything off in a healthy way rather than shutting it out. Whether it's listening to the birds, watching animals going past, seeing the water trickle and the clouds go over the mountains, experiencing the sun rise or feeling the rain come down, it's the only place where I do just one thing. When I leave, I feel six foot tall.

GORDON CAMPBELL GRAY

LOCH ETIVE

GORDON CAMPBELL GRAY is a hotelier and philanthropist. He founded an eco-conscious luxury hotel group which includes the award-winning Le Gray in Beirut, One Aldwych in London and The Merchant House in Bahrain. In 2019 Gordon created The Wee Hotel Company, which operates The Pierhouse Hotel in Argyll and The Three Chimneys in Skye. He works with multiple charities to promote sustainable travel and is currently a vice president of Save the Children.

All my life I've been travelling. I've lived in the Caribbean, Beirut, France, but nothing equals the Highlands of Scotland. And although a place doesn't have to be objectively attractive to be beautiful to you, I do love my home, which is in Argyll, near Loch Etive. It's a place so beautiful that wherever I am in the world, all I can think of is gates opening and going up to the house.

The arrival is all about the garden. I'm crazy about gardens, and my garden has a hundred flowers in a vulgar array of every colour you can imagine. It just blows my mind. I open the door and my two Labradors, Findlay and Flora, come out. They are my mates, and I just adore them. I need to live where I can scream, "Do you know how much I love you?" to my dogs without

anyone going, "He's mad!" – because I do love my Labradors, almost more than family, friends, anybody. I'm quite happy rattling around with just them.

The house itself is baronial style, with no neighbours and quite a few rooms. It's on the peninsula, so it's not a house with a front or a back. Out of every window you can see the spectacular water. I use all of the rooms all of the time. It has a library, a morning room and a beautiful drawing room with masses of windows. I like to think there's a bit of quality in my day if I move around, read in one and make an effort preparing meals in the kitchen.

It's wonderful when home is the best place you could ever be. I used to fly away on a

Sunday night thinking how much I wished I wasn't leaving. Still, once I was away and the wheels were up, I got excited. I'm a bit of an adventurer. Although I've always loved hotels, I found hotel school very uninteresting. I had to get away and paddle my own canoe.

I worked in London as a purchasing manager for a big hotel. Then in 1972, I saw the famine in Bangladesh and realised I had to do something. So I phoned Save the Children and said, "I'm not a doctor, but what can I do?" They needed someone to buy and distribute medicine. It was something I could easily manage, so I said yes. I left my job, took the role and was there in six weeks. It was the simplest thing I've ever done. I'd had a very comfortable life, and it made so much

sense for me to try and make a difference.

I lived there out in the field, working at the mouth of the Ganges with no running water and no electricity. I also spent many years in Morocco and Nicaragua, which is where I met and married my wife Carolyn. Then I started to anchor films in Ethiopia or Haiti to show at schools and encourage people to donate money. But one day I was in Nicaragua and there was flooding in Brazil. I was to go straight away. That's when I realised I was becoming a kind of disaster follower, and I didn't want that.

But all that had changed me. One of my everlasting memories was in Haiti after the earthquake. At one point, we were filming, and the buildings were just going down. We had to start over about six

times, because I just lost it thinking about the people in the rubble. Then we went to a tented community where the little kids were in school. They were all smiling in these shirts, ironed beautifully by their mothers, with charcoal and tissue paper. They were all so eager to learn.

Here in the West, I do get down-hearted when I see people complaining or kids not wanting to go to school, not realising how lucky they are. I think about the children in disaster zones, who, despite everything, dare to be happy. I used to go to Calcutta every month, which the writer Dominique Lapierre called "the City of Joy". I think that is very true. Despite all the suffering, it really is joyful. You'll see three kids playing happily in the mud with two lollipop sticks. It blows me away.

So when I returned to the hotel industry, continuing to work with Save the Children from abroad, I put into practice the things I believed in: kindness, respect and their power to influence the world. My experiences made me realise the importance of treating people well, and I've made a point of surrounding myself with this mindset and finding nice people who are enthusiastic. To be nice in its purest sense is a wonderful thing. Nice to each other and nice to guests. When I look at CVs, I want to find out if someone is kind – because we are in the business of kindness. If the staff aren't polite, then the whole hotel isn't worth a pound of beans.

My first hotel was The Feathers, in Woodstock, Oxfordshire. I inherited a chambermaid who'd worked in service since she

was twelve. She was seventy-five, and you would hear her singing away down the halls. She made being a chambermaid one of the most proud, dignified things. And that says it all. As a room attendant, you make a room beautiful. The guest comes, messes it all up and goes out. You've got two ways to look at that room: either "Oh God!" or "I'm going to make this place beautiful all over again". You can choose who you want to be.

I learned so much from my experiences with Save the Children, and I still do learn from my role there. It's a constant presence in my life. One day I'm talking to the chef about what we're going to do with the scallops, and the next we're in a meeting trying to figure out how to deal with the latest catastrophe. I've been asked how I can be a luxury hotelier and work for Save the Children. But it doesn't matter what you're doing – just do it nicely. That's the bedrock of success.

I think it makes life very balanced when you've been forced into the other side and seen what it's like. But I don't apologise about being particular when it comes to the ripeness of a nectarine in a hotel room or making sure there's a slice of lime within every ice cube that goes into a drink. I love those little details, and it just means that you take pride in what you do.

Having said that, I don't live in an immaculate house myself. It's a very clean house, but I live in organised chaos. I wouldn't let it happen for a minute in a hotel, but I think that's very healthy at home. I re-

member getting back to the house once and someone said, "My God, I think you've been burgled!" No, I'd left it like that! It's not perfect, but it's perfect for me. I get real visual pleasure just walking around and seeing things I love.

I've had such a social life. I've become a part of the community surrounding all of the hotels, and with fundraising, I'm endlessly going out. So knowing in the back of my mind that home is there, in total isolation, surrounded by nature, is the ultimate luxury. I adore walking through the gates into the garden and having the contrast between life as a hotelier, as an adventurer and as a traveller.

For many years I was always travelling in May when the garden is at its peak with azaleas and rhododendrons, and I always missed it. There are moments in life when you're reminded of what you should value, and I said to myself, *So why are you leaving?* After that, I moved my whole base from London to my house in Scotland. I vowed that I would always be there in May for this magic moment – and it's always stunning.

I sit on the terrace with my coffee and the dogs running around the garden and just contemplate. I watch every plant coming alive, and if I'm lucky, I can see the otters on their weekly visit too. If someone said nobody would ever visit me again, well, that's fine by me. To wake up in the morning and know I can stay in this house and not have anything in the diary, that is magic.

LINDA BAULD

NEWHAVEN HARBOUR

LINDA BAULD is Chief Social Policy Adviser for the Scottish Government and the first woman to hold the Bruce and John Usher Chair of the Usher Institute at Edinburgh University. During her long career she has invest-igated the impacts of drugs, alcohol, tobacco and obesity on health. After seven years as Cancer Research UK's Prevention Champion, Linda played an important part in Scotland's fight against Covid-19 and was awarded an OBE in 2021 for services to guiding the public health response and public understanding of Covid-19.

At its heart, Newhaven is a village really. It has been a fishing port since the 1480s and there is so much history surrounding this place. There are stories about huge whales brought up to Leith and tales of the fates of so many of the men and women who cultivated fish and oysters.

When I decided to move back to Edinburgh, I knew the choice was between buying a place near Newhaven Harbour or Granton pier a short walk away. I had never planned to go further than that, because this area is so full of memories for me.

I've been going to Newhaven Harbour since I was a little girl. My grandparents used to live on Laverockbank Road, a few minutes' walk from the shore. We used to wander around and then get fish and chips to eat on the pier. Then we emigrated to Canada when I was nine. Although I came back to do my PhD in Edinburgh and often returned to visit my family, I didn't come back to live in the north of the city for another twenty years.

I lived in Germany, France, Kent and Bath, but was continually drawn back to Newhaven because I love it. If I'm away in London or somewhere busy, I always look out for Newhaven when my plane is coming in to land. When I can see my special part of Edinburgh, it feels like coming home.

The image of Edinburgh – the castle and the places people are familiar with – doesn't always leave room for the other bits of the city that don't get the attention they deserve. The tourists leave the ship at Ocean Terminal and go straight to the

"When I can see my special part of Edinburgh, it feels like coming home."

centre of town. It would be brilliant to get more of them down here to Newhaven. Edinburgh is a port city, and this is a gorgeous place to take a wander.

I have thousands of pictures of the harbour. The sky is so open and changeable when the sun is rising, or at night, or at different times of the year. I've spent most of my life near water, and I love to see the whole vista, out to Queensferry and over to Fife. It's spectacular if it's clear.

Although it's changed over the years, the area is filled with memories of childhood and visiting from Canada. There are places like Mason's Bakery, which has been here since my mother was a child and is still open. The Starbank Inn and the park are at the bottom of my grandparents' road. As children we used to roll eggs down the hill at Easter and build snowmen in the winter months.

My grandmother's ashes are scattered at Granton Pier, as she used to love swimming in Wardie Bay. That's just what they did in those days, and it's lovely to see we've come full circle with open-water swimming. My aunt, who is over seventy, still goes swimming in there and she keeps trying to convert me. Unsuccessfully so far!

Some of my family are still in the same neighbourhood, so I can walk to their houses. On one of those walks when I first moved here, I discovered a gym. I'm a keen gym-goer, and this particular place has a big window where you can look out over the amazing views across the sea towards the bridges. It's a totally different experience to run or lift weights while you're looking out into this stunning scenery.

I watch the seabirds and the fishing boats sailing alongside the somewhat amusing little transit boats coming from the big cruise ships, with pipers serenading the guests off to catch the bus into town. I feel very grateful to have a life where I can do this, because not everyone is so lucky.

One of the things I like most about the harbour is that I can go there any time. It takes me about ten minutes to walk from the house, so I go downhill and see the Firth of Forth. It's also the key reason I chose this place to live. If you think about being active and having a moment to reflect, in an ideal world I would go to the Pentlands, to the west of Scotland, hillwalking, whatever. Those places are far away though, and it's an effort to get there. So living in a place where there are opportunities for promoting good mental and physical health near at hand is great.

I walk a lot. I aim for twelve to fifteen thousand steps a day, so that's my hobby. It always makes me feel reflective and relaxed. If I just need to get out of the house, I'll look out the window to see what the sky is like and literally just run down. It's in the opposite direction from work, so I associate this place with family time and free time. It's different to the home and office, and peaceful in a changeable way; it moves throughout the seasons so you can never get bored of it.

Green spaces, walking, just getting out should be accessible to all. That was a huge motivator when I was studying. I come from a medical family: my dad was a medic, my mum a nurse and my paternal grandmother was a nurse. Rather than studying medicine to diagnose people, I found a different route into it: prevention rather than treatment. I lived with my grandmother in Edinburgh whilst I was doing my PhD. She was a young nurse when the NHS was founded and we would talk about what a big step forward that was.

The environment is one of the fundamentals of the public health service. From the early years of sanitation and ventilation, and the change in living conditions that brought about, it's been about trying to improve health, especially for those with fewer resources.

Public health is like three circles. We have health protection for infectious disease; health improvement for stroke, heart disease and so on; then data and health informatics and health services. I come from the health improvement circle. That's my discipline.

My background is not about bacteria but about how you reduce exposure to environmental and behavioural risk factors: diet, smoking and things like that. If you study those, you realise there are huge inequalities and poverty is a major driver.

> *"Green spaces, walking, just getting out should be accessible to all."*

By studying public health, you can become quite passionate about social justice. The place or society a person lives in is interlinked with their health. I began to see it starkly when I started looking into studies on smoking and ageing. One of the biggest differences in health is whether people smoke or not, and currently in the UK we have more smokers in poorer areas.

So the most important thing someone can do for their health is to be born into an affluent family. All the experts – the people from my side researching socio-environmental factors, the people who diagnose disease, the scientists in the lab – will all tell you that. But of course where we're born is something that none of us can control.

That being the case, we need to think about well-being. The thing people can do that will make a difference is to value their health and realise they have autonomy in some aspects of it, even while others seem overwhelming.

We can take small steps to staying healthy near to where we are. Getting away from crowds and allowing activity, even only for a few minutes, and space and time to think: these are things we know will help to keep us healthy as we age.

Even though my own research is not about the built environment and green spaces, I'm very hopeful that one day everyone will have somewhere green or blue to go to. Whether ambling, swimming, sitting or running, finding a place that anyone can walk to that they find peaceful, and lovely, even in a modest sense, is incredibly important. In my own life, that's the most valuable resource that Newhaven Harbour gives me.

I've been back here for more than a decade, so I've made my own memories now. It's lovely for my children to have their teenage years living in the same part of Edinburgh that I know so well. I have a cousin who has visited from Australia and she loves the harbour too. She's even been persuaded to go into the water with my aunt. My kids, like me, decided against it. We're going to stick to a nice walk.

SUE LAWRENCE

ISLAY

SUE LAWRENCE rose to fame after winning the BBC's *Masterchef*. She has since published several popular cookbooks, written for *Scotland on Sunday* and the *Sunday Times* and appeared as a regular panellist on BBC Radio 4's *The Kitchen Cabinet*. In 2015, Sue began her successful career as a historical novelist. Her fictional novels highlight the challenges Scottish women in the past have faced in order to have their voices heard. These include the critically acclaimed *The Unreliable Death of Lady Grange*, *Down to the Sea* and *The Green Lady*.

There's something so special about Islay. It's the place where our family, just the five of us – my husband, myself and our three kids – have gone for years to get away from it all. A place where I can indulge my love of good Hebridean food. A place where the stones breathe such history that I started to consider a whole new career as a novelist too.

We first visited in 1990. I remember the kids seeing the ferry and being amazed that we were actually going into the bowels of the boat. It was a half-term holiday, and we'd borrowed the house in Ballygrant from a friend, not knowing that we were going to find ourselves in the middle of a heatwave. We had absolutely nothing with us: no shorts or T-shirts; not so much as a bucket or spade. But what we found was miles and

miles of stunning little hidden beaches which we went to every single day: the Singing Sands, Kilnaughton Beach and the first one we ever visited, Saligo Bay. That day I remember struggling down the sand, carrying my youngest child with the other two in tow, complete with picnic, to find we were the only ones there. Not a cloud in the sky and this glorious beach, empty apart from these huge cows strolling along. It was heaven!

My enjoyment of the island's food didn't come all at once. In the early days, people on Islay and other Scottish islands were a bit diffident about their wonderful local fare. I think they assumed that the crabs and lobsters they were fishing just for themselves weren't the sort of thing that visitors would want. It's not that they were ashamed of it; they just thought, *Why would anyone want to eat this?* Eventually, they realised how strong the demand was in France and Spain and that this was also exactly what visitors to the islands craved – the most fantastic, fresh, locally sourced produce you can find anywhere. This is a relatively recent development and it's true to say that travel has opened everyone's eyes, not just mine, and helped us all to appreciate what we have on our own doorstep.

Having been raised in Scotland, I was brought up on good plain food and excellent baking by my mum, but I've always loved eating and trying different cuisines. There was a time when, while living in France, Finland, Germany and Australia, I was discovering new food all the time and always asking people for recipes. My husband was working as a pilot at the time, and he would say, "I'm off to Brazil," or, "Do you fancy Venezuela?" and I would say, "Okay!" But instead of lounging by the pool I'd look for the Venezuelan *arepa* or visit the market in São Paulo, always on the hunt to find food wherever we went.

Then, after winning *MasterChef* in 1991, I'd go away on press trips to Buenos Aires, do a story on *dulce de leche* or visit Tokyo for the freshest sushi, which was *so* fresh it was almost quivering. I'd go to Iran to find pistachios, Turkey for apricots and discover entirely different

worlds whilst my husband would stay at home to look after the kids, who would groan and say, "Oh, is it Dad's pork casserole again?"

Gradually, during our visits to Islay, I began to learn how the island worked. These huge, refrigerated vans would be taking beautiful lobster and crab away on the ferry, off to Madrid or Paris. So I started negotiations with the fishermen. They would say, "No, no, it's all accounted for, can't do it," and I would ask, "Please could I just buy one little crab?" and eventually I persuaded them to sell me a couple. I remember the kids standing in the kitchen, looking on with half horror, half astonishment at me showing them how I got into the shell (which, con-sidering the mess, should have really been done outside, if not for the weather). Now we always have seafood on the first night of our holiday – it's a very special family tradition for us.

Later, I went back on my own, doing research for a book, discovering the only local butcher, chatting to those fishermen in Port Ellen. I went to meet an oyster man, and a farmer who gave me instructions to drive up this single track road. I was driving up in my bright-red hire car and there was an enormous bull in the middle of the road. *Well*, I thought, *I'm not going to do this*, and I reversed all the way back down and phoned him from the bottom. He said, "Oh it's fine, it's just the bull," and came

"We see the ferries and there's a lovely feeling of *we aren't going home yet.*"

and got him, but it was pretty terrifying when you weren't used to it. Still, the whole experience, it just reinvigorated my love for the island, getting to know the people, the best places to eat and the finest local produce.

There's also history everywhere. That started me thinking that perhaps I could get into writing fiction too. My first couple of fiction books still had a lot of food in them, which was the blend I needed to help me transfer from food to fiction. My next book takes place in Mull, Islay and Inveraray, so I always go and ask people how you get from here to there. And they make sure I get the details right, like whether it's a sandy or a stony beach. I write about women with no agency or power, who come good in the end. My husband keeps saying for once could you write about a nice man, but it was like that in those days and so tough for women. Perhaps I'm bringing them to the surface, giving them back their place.

When I went back for the 2012 Islay Book Festival, I was staying in a B&B, which I now know was at the south end of the island but at the time was surrounded by thick fog all weekend. I had no idea where I was going, but all the authors stayed cosy and sampled the local cafés, and we had such a lovely time. It reminded me of how much I cherish Islay. So a few years later I found a lovely house to rent on a perfect little beach near Port Ellen, and now we stay there every summer with my children and grandchildren, who love it.

On the first night at 5p.m., Ishbel from Islay's Seafood Shack arrives in a little van, bringing freshly cooked, dressed crab, langoustines, lobsters, whatever you want, usually still warm. We devour the platter with plenty of mayonnaise and beautiful artisan sourdough from Kirsty at the Island Bakehouse on Jura. It's honestly incredible.

After the little ones are in bed, we sit by the window in the conservatory, some of Emma's delicious Islay Cocoa chocolates to hand, and we look out on to the beach. It's like a framed painting. There's something so therapeutic and calming about the waves rolling in. We see the ferries and there's a lovely feeling of *we aren't going home yet*. You look out with binoculars for the otters, watch the swans bobbing about with their cygnets and look out towards the lighthouse. Nothing is rushed and everything is calm. It's the most relaxed I ever feel. No make-up, I haven't combed my hair, and I just don't care. The ultimate antidote to city life.

After visiting Islay from time to time over many years, we now go every single year and I know we'll keep going back. It's such a reassuring presence in our lives, and even when it rains, it's my perfect place.

CLIVE RUSSELL

LUNDIN LINKS BEACH

———————

CLIVE RUSSELL is a critically acclaimed television and film actor, known for his appearances as Brynden Tully in *Game of Thrones* and Chief Inspector Frederick Abberline in *Ripper Street*. He has also acted in a myriad of hit series and films, including *Still Game, Outlander, Sherlock Holmes, Silent Witness, Midsomer Murders* and *The Peripheral*.

Here we are on Lundin Links Beach. We're sitting on dunes, we're looking at the beach, we're in the long fescue grass and we're in a wind. The air moves so much when you're by the sea, and all the different ways it can move, for me, are quite extraordinary. It is very rarely calm. When you come out in winter, the rain turns to frost and stings you. You're completely alive at all times on a beach.

My whole life has been about beaches. I grew up in the town of Leven, two miles from here, and we came down to the beaches for picnics. We'd run down to this burn and we'd dam it up and make a loch. It would take all day, and the water would back up, and the golfers on the links would come to it and say, "What the f— do you think you're doing?" and we'd run off. In summer, I learned to swim in these waters, and in winter, we'd travel up through the ice and snow to come sledging on the golf course. This was our playground. Everything happened here.

One of the things I love about this beach is the land over by the horizon. When I was little, we lived next door to an English couple whose son was my pal. In the house, there were pictures of South Africa, where they had lived. This kid didn't have toy soldiers; he had toy animals. We played with lions and tigers and monkeys and all kinds of things. I was always fascinated by South Africa and the continent of Africa.

My granny had a flat looking across to Bass Rock one way and Dunbar the other way, and that was very intriguing. So I asked her, "Granny, where's Africa?" She said, "It's across the sea, laddie."

So I'm sitting by the window of her flat and I look out, and that for me was Africa. The idea that I could see Africa was thrilling and quite profound.

I've travelled all over the world, working as an actor or for whatever reason. But when I landed in Africa, it was one of the most enthralling moments of my life because I had already seen it from across that beach. And part of the excitement today is that a tiny bit of me still believes that Africa lies across this Fife coast.

All of those things fly back to me when I come here now. I remember beach parties when we were adolescents: low-level hedonism at best, but to us it was really, really bad and wild. Which felt fantastic. We would go to the sand dunes beyond the golf club, which were a lot bigger than they are now, taking the old heavy golfing umbrellas. We'd jump from the top and float down, then make a bonfire and camp along at Lundin Links by the pillboxes, these anti-tank stones you find all the way around the coast.

I was very self-conscious at one point as a teenager, being six foot six and covered in spots. I was very, very shy. This was a place to come and be safe. It was a place to be calm. It was about the rhythm and the sound and the smell of the sea. I've never forgotten that. It was a difficult time, but I could always come and sit on a rock, sit with the dog and feel free to think and reassemble myself and be occasionally wowed by the extraordinary difference when the sun is up in midsummer, and you can see the windows in North Berwick and the birds who come along, the herons, the gulls. It's extraordinary.

Then, in the sixties, when I was a student, coming back home, I used to deliver the Christmas post. We'd go along the East Neuk and St Monans, Pittenweem and Anstruther, which used to have huge fishing boats. With the collapse of the mining industry, I think unemployment and everything that goes with it – money problems, drug addiction – gave the places I grew up in a reputation for being a bit rough. But the town used to be thriving. And seeing the high street all boarded up, it's weird. You come back to a very different place from the Leven of the fifties and sixties I grew up in.

I saw a discussion between Tony Blair and Christopher Hitchens once, basically talking about God. Tony Blair was asked the question, "What is unique about your relationship with God?"

He answered, "I continue to have a sublime relationship with God." To which Hitchens replied, "I've had a sublime relationship with the woman I'm in love with. I have a sublime relationship at times with my children, with art, with paintings, with film, with landscape and seascape."

I've never bought into the idea of religion, but I don't think there's any question that there are moments of that sublime relationship for me here too.

In my view, happiness comes in moments, maybe minutes if you're lucky. Sublime moments in nature and seascape are

"I think you have to find places,
or a place, where you feel safe and
looked after, and that's what this
essentially is for me."

equally rare but equally profound. It's just you and what you see – and that's part of why this place is home to me. If I'm sitting here on my own, there's no photograph about to happen and I can just listen. I think because of the person I am, and my capacity to be set apart from other people and just enjoy my own company, I feel really free.

I do a lot more walking now than I did. You can walk all the way around the coast on the Fife Coastal Path, and there are few places that are far from a golf course or a village. There are some spots, particularly between Crail and St Andrews, where relatively few people walk far from the villages or the town. It has such a sense of remoteness you feel as if you're in the Western Isles. I layer up and have no problem being out in the cold. I love the feeling of rain and being stung by snow. I walk and pick things up and notice things. You see blue fisherman's gloves, creels from the lobster boats.

When I was a kid, I think I wouldn't have regarded this as being particularly beautiful. It was just where I lived. My mother encouraged me to get out of Scotland, so I did. But coming back to it, you go, *Wow!* You've got an adult perspective on everything. When my parents retired, they moved half a mile from here, and I now live eight miles away, and there are beaches everywhere. I walk on them all the time. Coming back, it's all changed – the boats are much smaller, the social stuff has changed too, but the beaches are eternal.

There are places in the world where I can go and be comfortable on my own. There's Luskentyre Beach on Harris, Talisker Beach on Skye, the fifty-mile beach on the North Island in New Zealand, beaches in Queensland, Nova Scotia, British Columbia. I enjoy being in these places because there's a beach, and as I grew up with this, I take all that with me.

I think you have to find places, or a place, where you feel safe and looked after, and that's what this essentially is for me. The relationship with what, I suppose, is a pretty hostile piece of stuff, the sea, reassures me. Its eternal nature comforts me, and I feel I'm at home. And I can always look across the sea and say to myself, *There's Africa.*

GEMMA LUMSDAINE

MONIFIETH BEACH

GEMMA LUMSDAINE plays and coaches at the Dundee Dragons Wheelchair Sports Club. She was named Sportscotland's 2018 Young Coach of the Year and played basketball for Scotland's U19 squad, before being invited to become part of the GB wheelchair rugby talent pathway, a programme designed to train the next generation of athletes to compete at the Paralympics. Gemma is on the Scottish Women and Girls in Sport advisory board and is Disability Lead at the young people's charity Sported.

My perfect place is Monifieth Beach. It's special for me because that's where I go to walk my dogs and relax. I'm an athlete, so I spend a lot of time travelling about and training. I often don't take time to do the simple things, as I have a habit of being quite blinkered in life, going one hundred miles an hour, one hundred per cent of the time.

I moved to Monifieth in Angus when I was six, so I've been here for nineteen years. When I first lived here, there wasn't a lot of attention given to physical accessibility. I never got to appreciate going out on the beach and walking the dogs until much later on in life, mainly because at that time I found it hard to embrace being a wheelchair user. It took a lot of courage for me to be able to go out and do normal things.

I remember one of the key moments that changed everything. It happened one Christmas Eve four or five years ago. My uncle and aunt came up with their dog. The sun was setting, and it was so stunning. I remember just being amazed and thinking, *Wow, I don't want to take this for granted.*

I live two minutes away from the beach, and I now love going down there, watching the dogs playing and seeing what's going on around me. My dogs are called Cooper and Millie. They are dad and daughter cocker spaniels who can't get enough of the beach. I'll grab a coffee from the wee van there (it feels great supporting a small business with my love of caffeine) and maybe even get a pup cup for the dogs too.

I work full-time for an amazing organisation called Sported, where we support young people within sport. Getting involved in disability sport was totally life-changing for me. Before then, I lacked confidence and really struggled to accept my disability. Sport helped me to find a purpose and a sense of belonging. It's what motivates me to support other people to experience those benefits.

The more I do, and the more I see, and the more I learn in this area, the more I realise how much needs to be done to move things forward – which is good, but equally it's a bit of a mountain to climb. I feel a responsibility to make change and influence people, especially those in my local area. Within my job and within everything I do, I have a role to play in terms of representing people who don't have a voice and don't have a platform.

I see young disabled people all the time who are just like me when I was younger, struggling with different challenges. To be able to use sport to support them and show them that actually they can do a lot and have a great future – that's what keeps me going. Thinking about some of the young people I work with . . . when we start working together, they don't push the chairs themselves and they'll always look for help. Then, as time goes by and we keep at it, they gain independence and become a lot more empowered. It's brilliant to see the ways in which we're helping them go so far beyond sport.

A lot of people think that taking part in sport, especially recreational sport, is about going in, doing some exercise, playing a game, then leaving. But actually it's a key tool that makes a huge impact on people's entire lives, particularly on the lives of those with disabilities. It's about your whole life, your whole independence. And you can take that confidence anywhere.

Recently, I went to Moray with the Dundee Dragons, the local sports club I'm involved in, to try adapted surfing for the first time. Seeing the sense of freedom in everyone and being able to be in the water for the first time was remarkable. There was a young person with us who often doesn't show a lot of emotion. It was incredible, that whole day, to see that they just couldn't stop smiling. That will stay with me forever. It reminds me of why I do what I do, and the significance of it.

Day to day, it's easy to lose track of what you're working towards. For a lot of non-disabled people, it would be trivial to go surfing or play a sport, but for us it's genuinely life-changing. There are so many barriers and challenges and, I think, achievements. Even just seeing a little bit of progress reminds me of the reason why we do things and why society and sport need to continue moving forward.

I sometimes get these moments for myself too, as an athlete and a player. Last month, we went out to Paris with the GB rugby

"It's easy to underestimate the power of having accessible spaces to explore . . . places where all communities can feel accepted."

"I lacked confidence and really struggled to accept my disability. Sport helped me to find a purpose and a sense of belonging."

team. Rugby is a very male-dominated sport, but this was a women-only tournament, and the first time GB had ever put a women's team in. It was amazing! We got out there and won the whole thing. But for me, the most special thing was to be a part of that history, alongside a new culture and the feeling of women supporting each other.

I think it's crucial for people to have that support and to do something that means a lot to them, whether it's taking part in physical activity or going out in the fresh air. It's easy to underestimate the power of having accessible spaces to explore. And by this I mean places where all communities can feel accepted: people with different abilities, minorities and women too. Intersectionality is a huge thing, and I feel very strongly that we need more awareness of that as well. If you're a disabled woman from a diverse community, you will have even less access to those spaces. I'm really passionate about making that happen for everyone.

It's not something that I feel is an external pressure. I'm definitely the one who's taken this on myself. But I am terrible at

taking breaks. I'm just going to say that outright. Most days, I spend the majority of my time either at the desk or training, and sometimes I just need to step away.

I'm very thankful that I have a good circle of friends and family around me, who are amazing at showing me the importance of supporting my own mental health. They'll say, "It's okay to do nothing," or "You can take the dogs out for a walk – you don't need to be doing everything all at once." So I look out of the window, and if it's a nice day, or I have a day off, I find a family member or friend and we'll go to Monifieth beach.

Going to the beach gives me the opportunity to leave my phone at home and remember how important it is to have the time to do something at a slower pace. I can achieve a lot with my mindset, but as much as it's a skill to train and be an athlete and do all this other stuff, equally it's as great a skill to slow down and rest.

I was there on the beach last week. The sun was shining and it felt like the most peaceful moment ever. I feel so endlessly lucky to have this place on my doorstep.

GORDON &
VANESSA QUINN

BADACHRO

GORDON & VANESSA QUINN are entrepreneurs with a shared passion for a more peaceful way of life. The couple met at the Badachro Inn and ran a successful B&B together for many years. In 2017 they decided to combine Gordon's advertising background with Vanessa's previous work in horticulture, opening Badachro Distillery. There they create rare whiskies, gins and vodka using local botanicals, and run Little Aird Hill, which offers accommodation surrounded by stunning panoramic views across to Skye and beyond to the Outer Hebrides.

Gordon: Badachro in the north-west Highlands is our home and our favourite place. It's a cove on the mainland coast opposite the most northerly point of Skye – a little hidden bay that connects to the sea. It gives you a very special feeling of being nestled.

Vanessa: Definitely. It feels as if it's hugging you. We're incredibly lucky to live in the place that, coincidentally, is perfect for us both. I first came to Badachro on a school trip a long time ago and then studied in Edinburgh. I kept coming up here to meet friends, and eventually I met Gordon.

Gordon: I used to come up often with one or two pals to spend a bit of time walking.

I was drawn to this place initially because if I was feeling any hint of melancholy, Badachro was always an antidote. It's a very rugged, wild, dramatic landscape, with mountains and sea and lochs. It's one of the most beautiful places in the world.

Vanessa: We're slightly biased – but it is! We fell in love with the place independently of each other, and we ended up having the same friendship group and were introduced in the pub.

Gordon: Both us were attracted by the landscape but also by the people we met here, who were really warm. There were fishermen chatting to top lawyers and chief executives, a rock star drinking with the binman. Everyone was having these completely natural, warm conversations about everything. In fact, one of the first conversations Vanessa and I had when we were introduced was about how eclectic the mix of people was in Badachro. That was twenty-six years ago now.

Vanessa: And we got married twelve weeks later!

Gordon: Yes, and I wasn't terribly romantic with my proposal. I used to run part of the advertising for Pepsi, and they would move me around from market to market. Just before I proposed, I was offered a job in the Middle East. We had fallen in love with each other of course, but I knew that as a single female, Vanessa wouldn't be able to come to Saudi Arabia and live on her own.

So I said, "Look, we either have to split up, meet four weeks a year when there are holidays, or get married and you come with me. What do you think?" Personally I preferred the last option. She said she wanted to think about it.

Vanessa: But I didn't think for too long.

Gordon: No, thankfully you didn't.

Vanessa: We got married in January, and Gordon moved to Saudi at the beginning of February, while I was still finishing university. We met a few times, but it was certainly a very strange thing to be greeting your husband at the airport.

Gordon: Especially in Saudi, where you can't hug. We used to meet with a quick,

sneaky handshake and that was it. Living in Saudi Arabia together was very interesting though, because neither of us could run away from anything: we had to be a very cohesive unit.

Vanessa: Even then people would say to us, "You've been together so briefly." Or, "This is either going to work forever or you're going to be out of here within months."

Gordon: But we stayed together. Then we decided to move to London. Just after we came back, I suffered from depression. I was good at getting big well-paid jobs but not very good at dealing with the pressure that came with them. It made us think long and hard about a few things, and we decided that London life really wasn't

working. There was just far too much stress. So that provoked a few changes.

Then we started thinking it might be nice to start a family. And we wanted to bring the kids up somewhere they had the outdoors and real roots, rather than a money- or career-focused lifestyle.

Vanessa: So in the end, we decided to move to the middle of nowhere! I was quite nervous about moving up here at first, because I was worried it was going to rub the gold off and take away that layer of shine that made Badachro so special.

I look back now and realise that when we moved here, there really was nothing. I mean, we literally had a meadow. We put

"Our family was telling us we were both totally nuts, but it was the best thing we ever did."

> *"Here we can get on with our work, then jump in the boat for an hour and go for a spin."*

a caravan on it and moved in with a baby and toddler, a puppy and an extremely grumpy cat. Then we started building the house by ourselves.

Our family told us we were both totally nuts, but it was the best thing we ever did. The idea was that it was going to be a much more relaxing life, in which both of us would always have each other's back. I think that's something we've been able to achieve.

I had my time off when the kids were little, but I always wanted to work. We opened a bed and breakfast, and we were able to make sure that one of us was functioning fully, even if we were really busy up here or if Gordon got overwhelmed by his job in those stressful environments. But you do have to work on it.

At one point, we nearly sold up, because when the kids were at school and I was running the bed and breakfast and Gordon was frequently away in Glasgow for his job, I was on my own a lot of the time. I began to think, *Is this the rest of my life?* I looked around and found an incredible place just outside Edinburgh to convert into a hotel. I persuaded Gordon to go

along with the idea and we actually did put the house on the market. But a good friend of ours came to stay with his family around that time and he kept on saying to me, "You're totally mad. This is your perfect place; this is your dream. Even before you met Gordon, this is where you wanted to be."

Then we watched the movie *Local Hero* with its beautiful seascapes. I remember the two of us waking up in the morning and just looking at each other. I looked at Gordon and said, "I don't think I want to move any more."

And Gordon said, "Me neither."

So even with a perfect place, you have to be prepared that it might not feel so perfect at times. But that doesn't mean it's not going to be right for you in the end.

I think doing the bed and breakfast for thirteen years together is what gave Gordon a chance to heal. In that time, the giant re-awoke in him. Now we have the distillery here, and it's Gordon's marketing and advertising background that has taken it to the level it's at now.

Gordon: I remember in the beginning walking along the road to my next-door neighbour and telling him over coffee that we'd decided to start a gin distillery. It was a case of, "Yeah, yeah, right, Gordon. Yeah, sure."

But we've done it. It's successful and we make a decent living here. We're never going to get rich, but we have a comfortable, pretty low-stress life in a beautiful place, and we're aware of how fortunate we are. Here we can get on with our work, then jump in the boat for an hour and go for a spin and maybe have a glass of wine on the beach.

Vanessa: And in winter there might not be many people around, but I love that hibernation feeling. There's a lot of just sitting by the fire and reading or watching a movie. You feel like you're really restoring yourself and nature is doing the same.

Gordon: Yes, because everything is done in west coast time. Everything is a bit slower. It's a bit "inshallah" here: everything in its own time; we'll be fine. It's been incredibly calming. I'm not religious in any formal way, but there is something very deep and moving that's good for the soul about this environment.

And we are really lucky that twenty-six years later, we're still happy and wouldn't change a thing. We came here not knowing each other and went from being two single people to a couple to a family of four.

Vanessa: And now we're back to two. Both our kids had a fantastic childhood until about the age of fourteen, when this turned into the most boring place in the whole universe. Now they're slowly starting to realise it's actually amazing. So they come back with their friends because they want to show it off. I love that they have this safety net of Badachro to recharge in and take a deep breath.

Gordon: And they've made it very clear that we're not allowed to sell the house. Ever. Which is good because we have no intention of doing so.

RHONA CAMERON

18 Grindlay Street

RHONA CAMERON is a writer, comedian and actor, who has appeared on programmes such as *Have I Got News for You*, *Never Mind the Buzzcocks* and the first series of *I'm a Celebrity Get Me Out Of Here*, which won a BAFTA and Rhona a television award. She had sell-out shows for decades in the Edinburgh Fringe, after winning Channel 4's *So You Think You're Funny* award in 1992. Rhona is the author of *1979: A Big Year in a Small Town*, a memoir which she has recently adapted for screen, and *The Naked Drinking Club*. She is writing her third book and developing various projects for television and film.

I have had a very difficult relationship with Scotland. It has mostly been a place of great trauma for me. The statistics of poor mental and physical health I see here need to be addressed. Surprisingly, I have been based here for the last few years due to my mother's decline, the pandemic and her death, which has been the hardest thing I have ever experienced.

However, the first seven years – apart from the adoption at the very start – is my version of perfect. I was taken from the unmarried nursing home in Dundee to Edinburgh at three months old by my new parents, Jean and Bill, beginning my life in a ground floor flat at 18 Grindlay Street and living there until I was seven, when they decided to move to parochial Musselburgh in East Lothian.

Grindlay Street was a time of safety and security, something I have been lacking since. It was a time before I knew I was adopted – which is key. It was a very old-fashioned, simple existence in a post-war extended family set-up. I would wake to the sound of the milkman's horse-drawn cart on the cobbles. It was a million miles away from the robots and computers of today.

I went to a nice nursery down the Royal Mile, then Tollcross Primary where I flourished. My dad, who was a mechanic, worked just round the corner. My gran lived opposite us, so when my mum went back to work, my gran would look after me. I played up and down the street on my little tricycle singing, "I was born under a wandering star" over and over after seeing the film *Paint Your Wagon*. I was known for this in the neighbourhood. I would shout up, "Gran, Gran!" and she would come to the window and lift it, waving and shouting, "Hello!"

In the mornings I would get into Mum and Dad's bed. I've always had sleep problems, but they had this little electric clock that would tick gently. This and the warmth from their bodies would make me feel safe and sleepy. During that period in Grindlay Street, life felt full of possibilities. It had security and love, not rage, violence, heartbreak or mistrust.

After we left and moved to Musselburgh, everything changed. At first, we had to live in a caravan because of a builders' strike. I started getting bullied and called "Gypo" and things started to unravel. Cancer would take my dad a few years later, leaving my mum and me under a lot of stress, which caused our relationship to deteriorate. One by one people who meant everything to me died, and with all these troubles I couldn't build any inner foundations.

The death of my father devastated me and older men in the background took advantage of my vulnerability. My lesbianism was an anomaly back then. I was treated very badly, which added to the mix and affected my ability to concentrate. I was a gifted painter, which at least provided solace, and my portfolio was accepted to Edinburgh College of Art, but I failed my academic qualifications so I couldn't go. I left home poorly

equipped for the world, drinking, doing menial jobs and going from one woman to another.

I did, however, keep writing in my many notebooks, performing my poetry, and doing a bit of acting in political theatre. I started doing stand-up in London among a group of genius oddballs and we had the freedom to do and say what we pleased on stage. I gained success quickly and was consumed by a comedian's lifestyle. Back then it was proper gigs in smoky clubs, with riotous late nights at the Fringe, the Comedy Store and Gilded Balloon at three in the morning.

Despite loving the autonomy, I've always felt an ambivalence towards stand-up, because at the same time as it made my name and launched me into the arts, it was just another thing that became bad for me. For my body, for my soul, for my mental health and addiction, everything.

So when I had the chance to get easier, bigger money to do a game show, I jumped at it. But a lot of the stuff I ended up doing on TV wasn't me. I took those jobs because in those days it was hard to get well-paid mainstream work as a lesbian, and I became the first one on British television with my own show.

Essentially I'm a storyteller and a late developer. It just so happened that my need for self-authentication that came with ageing and its catalogue of losses, coincides with a time in history where people are finally understanding trauma.

This journey can't be undertaken with alcohol. I have been sober for a few years.

Growing up I had one foot in the old world. It was very regimented and there were no emotional dialogues with adults. Our parents and grandparents were shaped by the war and the post-war period. My parents' generation were often physically punished by their parents and at school, so they did the same to us. Outside, we were very un-policed, so there was lots of physical and sexual bullying, certainly for me.

My generation fought for the new freedoms too. We paved the way for LGBT people. When I first became a comedian, all I got asked about was, "How did you first know you were gay?", "Have you always been gay?" Now we don't have to define that to the press. I'm proud I was a warrior, but it was a lot to bear alone.

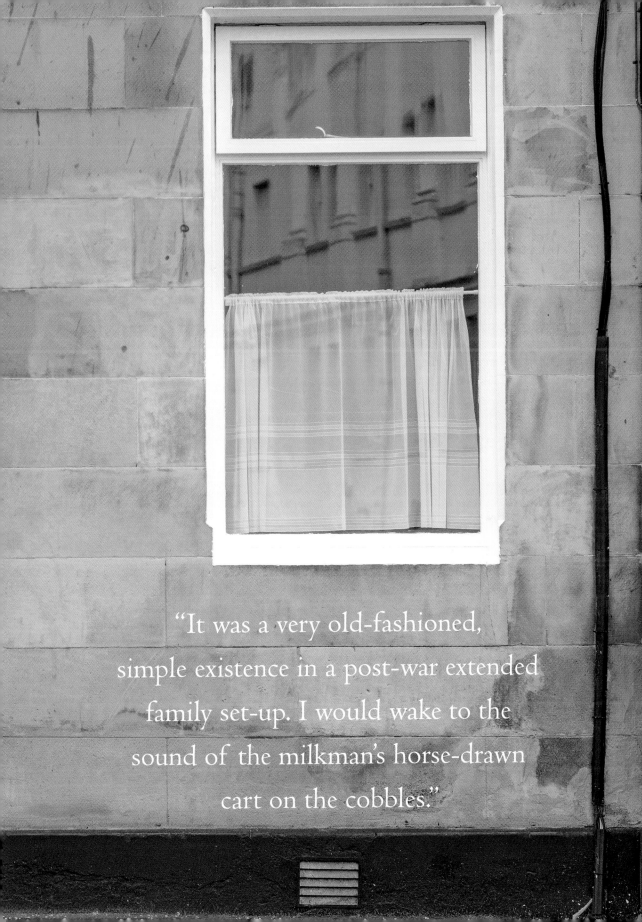

"It was a very old-fashioned, simple existence in a post-war extended family set-up. I would wake to the sound of the milkman's horse-drawn cart on the cobbles."

You've got to understand the link between your experiences, your trauma and your behaviours. We owe it to ourselves to do a process of self-enquiry. I haven't written a memoir for twenty years, though I recently adapted my first one, *1979*, for screen. This year in particular, being back here in Scotland, I have all this stuff in my head all the time. Since I've started writing it all down, I'm much more peaceful and can feel the healing and acceptance starting.

We're told not to be negative, to go where the light is. But sometimes light is found in darkness. I don't fear dark places or experiences, so that's when I come into my own. Which is why, when I was thrown into my mother's death, I was able to go with it and do the last stages of caring for her at home and holding her while she left.

I met a very wise astrological counsellor called Diana who said to me, "Remember, Rhona, you have to mine the shit for gold!" I have done a lot of therapies along the way. Psychoanalysis was illuminating but most therapy models are too concerned with labels. Sure, attachment disorder has a big part to play in those of us who did not have our emotional needs met. But for me an esoteric path has provided me with a broader understanding of my psyche.

Now I'm starting that process of rebirth, stepping into a new version of life. Though it's daunting; I'll be letting go of my childhood home of fifty years in Musselburgh. I work hard at staying healthy now. I eat well and I look after my body which has been through the wringer. And if I don't write or protect myself from the craziness out there, I perish.

I have a little soul dog called Brody, who keeps my heart open. I smile at him in the morning, no matter how bad I feel. He's been my little buddy in this house after my mum died: my little warm beating heart that I pull towards me in the morning. I have an extra hour of sleep with him, like I did with my parents in Grindlay Street before the bad times.

Back then we used to visit Goldbergs, a real old-fashioned store with a sweeping staircase of glass and money that travelled above the tills through pipes in the ceiling. It was enormous and all the families would visit to see the lavish Easter, Halloween or Christmas displays. I remember coming home with my gran and my mum from another lovely time, sitting behind the plastic of my pram and watching the raindrops. We got soaked in a downpour, so Mum put me in a warm bath.

On the lane now you'll see a boarded-up window, but in those days it was opaque. I would lie in the bath and watch the shadows of people going by. I think about these warm feelings in every bath since.

"Remember the good times," my mum said to me. She was a more optimistic person than I am. But she'd agree that most of our "unpolluted" good times were in that ground floor flat at Number 18 Grindlay Street.

DANNI MENZIES

LOCH TAY

DANNI MENZIES is a TV and radio presenter who became a household name whilst presenting Channel 4's *A Place in the Sun*. She has made appearances on *The Challenge* and *Celebrity Mastermind* and hosts a weekly show on Hoxton Radio. Danni works with many charitable organisations, including Home Kitchen and Shelter, and used her background in design to launch the interiors collection Menzies At Home, which supports the work of the homeless charity, The Soup Kitchen.

Loch Tay is so beautiful that it's easy to talk about. My perfect place is the point where the loch turns into the river. This is the place I always come back to when I want to switch off and unwind. It's calm and peaceful. The scenery is incredible. Being next to the water feels really good for the soul too. It's a calm, safe, comforting place, and I love coming back here to unwind after travelling.

The first thing I do the moment I get out of the car is just stand and breathe. The air smells and tastes so different out here. A few minutes away from my parents' house, there's a little forest path, where I usually walk alongside the loch and come out by the bridge at Kenmore. Then you can wander over the little bridge and down through the gorgeous village, head to the beach and sample some of that fresh air.

I grew up around Loch Tay and lived here for most of my life, before moving to London to pursue a career in television. When I was young, my mum used to take us down to the beach and make a wee fire. My granny used to come along, too, and sit on her wee chair. We'd all sit around this fire and have our dinner and watch the sun go down. Then, when we got older and my sister and I became naughty teenagers, we'd go down and make fires ourselves, jump off the rocks on the island and get up to all sorts. I also rode horses when I was younger, so in the summer, I would take the horses down to the beach, to cool off and have a swim.

The best thing about Loch Tay is that I've grown up here for twenty years and I'm still finding new places. There's a wealth of history and walks in the area, and always something to do, which I think is

> "Going down to the beach and having supper used to be a run-of-the-mill activity, but now it's something I cherish."

remarkable for such a small place with not too many people in it. The landscape is always the same, but the big difference for me as an adult is that I'm now so much more grateful for this place.

Going down to the beach and having supper used to be a run-of-the-mill activity, but now it's something I cherish and want to keep as a memory forever. When I'm coming home, it's with a new sense of appreciation for the nature I grew up in that I just didn't have before moving to London, where it's hard to find any large outdoor spaces. Now when I visit, I feel I need to get out and experience everything that this place has to offer.

I've always had quite a sense of adventure, so if I manage to get my hands on a bit of kit, it's easy to pass the day doing lovely things outside. I go and run up the hills. (Sometimes you can even hike up there and ski down.) I'll get on a mountain bike with my dad, take a paddleboard out on the loch and make the most of every minute I can spend here. There are quite a lot of days I spend on my own too, just me and the dogs walking. Then I come back and we put the pizza oven on and get the family round to sit outside and have dinner looking out on the loch.

When I was here over lockdown, I did things I've never done, such as cold-water swimming with my auntie, who's part of a group called the Frozen Fannies. I'm so impressed by the way these women go out in the winter every day. After reading up and learning about the health benefits, I decided to be brave and give it a go. I really enjoyed the boost it gives you. While battling the cold is definitely exhausting, you're rejuvenated at the same time.

There's so much you can do here without going anywhere at all, but one of the things I love the most is taking a nice long drive. I find that quite therapeutic, just looking out of the windows and taking it all in. I think it's important for your sanity to reconnect with nature and breathe.

This place has been so helpful in my life, especially after I had an accident and was off work for a few months. I felt rubbish and couldn't go to the gym every day the way I'm used to. But I ended up finding that mental space in other ways and started meditation. It can seem quite scary at first, thinking you've got to sit cross-legged and hum or whatever.

"It's calm and peaceful. The scenery is
incredible. Being next to the water feels
really good for the soul."

I started by just typing into YouTube whatever I felt I needed: you know, "Twenty-minute meditation to relieve anxiety". Or I'd find things on the Calm app so that I could just sit, be still and listen. Being around the loch complements that kind of self-healing. Taking time to remove ourselves from the complications of modern life, to reflect and ask questions of ourselves is something we don't do enough of nowadays.

Something I also find incredibly helpful when I'm home is to take time to write what I think I need to hear – some affirmations. If you're feeling a certain way, you just write down the opposite. Whatever your inner voice is telling you to make you feel bad, write the antithesis down and just keep telling yourself that, every single day.

My inner voice was telling me, *You're getting lazy, you're eating rubbish, you're unfit.* I was beating myself up about not being able to do something that usually makes me feel good. So instead, I wrote down, "You are fit and healthy." Even though I wasn't feeling it, I said it to myself every morning. Naturally, I started making better choices and doing more, tricking my brain into thinking I already was the person I wanted to get back to, the person I want to be. Through doing this, I realised that the voice in my head is really important, and I have to look after it and make sure it's telling me the right things.

If you're struggling, it's important not to expect instant transformation. It's really hard, but truly fundamental, to focus on gradually replacing unhealthy habits with healthier ones and creating more consistent change over time. Eventually, you will do it.

For example, when I was living alone and had the evening to myself, I might find myself thinking about having a drink. So I would start to plan things to fill my time instead, like going to a yoga class. Eventually, I would find I had loads of things on which were making me feel really good, rather than allowing habits that would fuel bad feelings. Whenever I don't feel like it, or I'm in a rubbish mood, I say to myself, *Dress up and show up – just show up.* I can guarantee that the moment I walk out of that door, my energy will have undergone a complete shift.

In London, or when I'm travelling around for work, there aren't many places I go where I can just put down my phone. Life is always so busy, thinking of this thing and planning for the next. But out by the river, or on a long, aimless drive at home, I've left my phone behind for the day. I don't care if anyone calls or gets in touch – I'm completely out of reach.

Having somewhere you can go to switch off completely helps you to balance yourself out again. That freshness, the quiet, the stillness. When I'm home on Loch Tay and come back after being out in the fresh air for the day, I feel such a different level of calm and contentment. I always go to bed and fall into deep, beautiful sleep. I sleep as if I haven't slept in a year.

SHAUNA MACDONALD

PORTOBELLO BEACH

_____

SHAUNA MACDONALD is a Scottish actor, known for her starring roles in the classic horror film _The Descent_ and the hit spy drama _Spooks_. In 2018 Shauna won Best Actress in the Film category at the BAFTA Awards Scotland for her role in _White Chamber_ and she has also appeared in _Star Wars: The Last Jedi, Shetland_ and _Outlander_. Shauna is the co-artistic director of the award-winning Edinburgh Youth Theatre, which helps young people find confidence through the performing arts.

My perfect place is Portobello Beach. I grew up in Portobello, and there's a gravity that pulled me back. My family home is a thirty-second walk from the sea. I would be out there in the buggy and then walking and toddling into the sea.

When we were in primary school, I was a really shy kid with a lisp. I had a big sister who would do all the talking, so that worked well for me. I was so awkward. I just didn't like speaking, because people would laugh at me. So my mum, bless her, kept trying to make me go to things, like amateur dramatics, which I hated because it was all about who was the loudest.

I remember lots of fetes and gala days, where they would use the promenade for Victorian dress days and community events. At one point the pool was going to

close, so all the kids and their mums and dads got together and petitioned. We had signs saying "Save Our Pool".

Then when I was older in high school, I remember the promenade always at night, always dark. I was trying to get home before Mum and Dad realised I wasn't there, or to find the dark place in which to do things I probably shouldn't be doing. So as a kid, Portobello was full of bright sunny days, and as a teenager, it was dark and bitterly cold but quite exciting.

At that point I started travelling to a Brunton Youth Theatre in Musselburgh and the Paisley Youth Theatre. They would do productions of _The Tempest_ or _Earth Crack_ about the Greek gods. James McAvoy and David Sneddon and all these amazing actors were my friends, but at that time we were just a bunch of people who were passionate about theatre. It was a really exciting environment, and I fell in love with the joy of playing and the fact that you didn't have to be the loudest person in the room.

When I was sixteen, I got a part in a film called *The Debt Collector*. I used to clean for someone called Eric Coulter, whose sister was an amazing agent called Anne Coulter. She took me on board, and luckily I didn't do very well in my Highers other than in Drama and English, so it was an easy decision to become an actor.

I lived in Portobello until I was eighteen and then all I wanted to do was leave. So I did. I went to Glasgow for three years to drama college, which I loved. And then I went down to London for almost four

years. It was a really busy time for work and travelling. But I decided to move back here because I wanted to start a family and it was just a no-brainer because of the amazing childhood I'd had. Also the emotional call was to be home with my mum and my dad, living that life but still acting.

At the time, I had to make a bit of a sacrifice in terms of career trajectory, but really I just wanted to have a happy life. I wanted my children to be happy, and I knew that on the beach they could grow up with their extended family around.

I've done a lot of films in the horror genre, so I'm quite lucky that if I'm not covered in blood, nobody knows who I am! I think I'm more recognised because

I run Edinburgh Youth Theatre. I run it with Jo Jeffries, who is a great childhood friend of mine, and we have more than two hundred kids every week. We've also started Scottish Youth Cinema School. I wanted something that all the local kids and beyond could come to that was a safe space; that was creative and inclusive and accessible; and that young people could explore with their peers and develop their own voices.

I've had the joy of creating that space, which wasn't here when I was young. So I'm recognised as the woman who does the drama rather than the girl off the horror films. I've got a bit of a split personality going on, because I still do loads of work like that as an actor while also teaching kids in the theatre.

I once took ten of my youth-theatre kids to see the film I won the BAFTA for, *White Chamber*, which was showing at the Edinburgh Film Festival. I forgot the movie was a certificate fifteen. I knew there was nothing explicit in it – just a wee bit of blood – but I sat in that cinema thinking, *Ohhh, forgot about that bit. Oh God, am I going to get emails in*? But by the end they were saying, "Shauna, that was so cool!"

The beach can be a bit scary sometimes. There's a tradition here that families get together and all the kids rush into the sea. There have been a couple of times when I've been fully clothed, swimming out to "save" a child. Then I get to the child and they're totally fine. I do find the sea quite intimidating, although I don't think it's an unhealthy fear. The sea has got a power

"The beach feels like an extension of me. I always say I'm from Portobello. Not Joppa, not Edinburgh, but Portobello."

> *"Portobello attracts people, because once you're here, you stay."*

we can't fight. If it wants to take us, we get caught up in it, and that's it.

It makes you very aware of how small and insignificant you are. You go down to the beach and you've got this vastness of sky and the vastness and darkness of the ocean. My little problem, or my anxiety, or whatever is holding me back doesn't really matter in the grand scheme of things. I'm a very small part of this massive beast that is, you know, the world. So it's very grounding.

The beach feels like an extension of me. I always say I'm from Portobello. Not Joppa, not Edinburgh, but Portobello. Once you live in a seaside community, it becomes a kind of village green, I guess. You're constantly making connections with people. Although there's maybe a Groundhog Day going on, because now my kids look like a carbon copy of me and my sister. We even went to the same primary school. Portobello attracts people, because once you're here, you stay. And you invest in the community because it's so special.

The kids I grew up with are still in Portobello: they left and came back because they've got the same draw to the sea and the community as I do. So you want everything to stay the same, but you don't realise that until something's taken away from you. My mum died last year, and I found it really tough to be in any space that she used to go to and to see the friends of hers who remind me of being free and happy and a kid.

But I do go to the promenade for respite and peace now. I feel that if I'm in any doubt of anything, of who I am and what's happened to me, I can come and remind myself. I'm not one for sitting and looking out at the sea; I always have to walk alongside it and process stuff. It's healing in some way. It feels like my absolute reality. I can't get away from it, so I accept it and I respect it.

If you loop the beach, walking to one end and back is about three and a half miles. It's very meditative. There's a gravity that sort of draws you too. Something about the quality of the air, because it's got the water and air from the sea. Something, too, about the sound when you're closer to the shoreline, the laughing of the waves. It's like breathing.

VAL McDERMID

St Monans

VAL McDERMID is one of the world's foremost crime writers, having sold over 19 million books in more than forty languages. Her most famous series, *Wire in the Blood*, was adapted into a hit TV show, while two popular crime dramas, *Traces* and *Karen Pirie*, are also based on her work. In 2008, Val was a judge for the Man Booker Prize and she is currently the lead vocalist for The Fun Lovin' Crime Writers, who have performed at the Glastonbury Festival.

My perfect place is my home on the East Neuk of Fife, right on the coast in St Monans. The windows look out towards the sea like paintings. So, first thing in the morning, I get up and look out of my bathroom window to this gorgeous scenery. That's what starts my day, even if I'm tired or fed up. Seeing that view of the sea and East Lothian in the distance, my worries are gone. I sit at my table with a wee cup of coffee and then I wander down to the office and start writing.

My office looks directly out to the sea, so it gives me plenty of inspiration for writing too. I've been inadvertently using the Pomodoro Technique for years. I write for twenty minutes or so at a time, then I get up and go outside, tinker in the garden or do whatever needs to be done and take a moment to look at the sea. I go back to writing and the day goes forward in chunks. You can see the time passing from what the sea is doing and watch the weather from far away. It's easy to tell where the wind is coming from: it's all down to whether you can see Berwick Law or not. There are sheets and circles of light that travel on the water, and as the light moves alongside the clouds, you can see gannets, shags and Cuddy's ducks (the local term for eider ducks). There's also the occasional heron or curlew and sometimes dolphins or minke whales.

I grew up down the coast from here, so as long as I can remember, this is the sea I've known. I've always found that being around water, especially moving water, is something that centres me, especially when I'm doing something creative. My favourite water is the sea. I suppose it plugs into a sense of belonging, a sense of a landscape I'm very familiar with. I think in terms of places to live in the world,

St Monans is one of the best. This is due to the stunning coast on our doorstep but also the lack of a pub, which means the tourists don't really hang around. We get the best of both worlds: the fabulous view of the sea and some peace.

We used to come up a lot to the East Neuk when I was a kid. On Sunday afternoons, we would drive and explore Fife, because my dad had a great penchant for going places he'd never been. We were once rescued from a snow-filled ditch by a farmer because my dad thought the single-track road up a hill in January looked interesting. We used to come up to the East Neuk, Anstruther, Crail, everywhere. I think I first visited St Monans specifically when I was quite small. My best

pal's mum came from here and brought us back regularly, so that makes it part of my roots too, I suppose.

It's always had a sense of difference, Fife. Although on one side it has Edinburgh and the other Dundee, it's neither of those. Really, until the sixties, when they built the road bridges, it wasn't straightforward to get here and it felt quite separate. At one point they planned to cut it across the middle and give one part to Edinburgh and one part to Dundee. Of course that caused a huge outcry and a campaign – I remember having a "Fight for Fife" badge on my school blazer. We knew we were different here in the Kingdom, with our own distinct identity. People have always been quite inclined to notice things around

here. They take nothing for granted and tend to question the status quo.

It was Fife that sent the first communist MP to parliament, and there's always been a sense of standing up for yourselves and not taking any rubbish. My dad was very much like that, a proud member of the Bowhill People's Burns Club, of which I am now lucky enough to be honorary president. I think my way of looking at the world was shaped through his eyes and through the poetry of Burns, with a sense of egalitarianism and "a man's a man for all that". I grew up feeling capable of doing anything I wanted. The only thing that could stand in my way was myself. I guess I ended up with a slightly bolshie attitude, which I think is quite common around here.

The reason I'm a writer is because of the Scottish public library and state education system. I came from a working-class mining family and there was no money to spend on university. My parents were both bright people, so they understood that pursuing education was important and gave me the best chance of succeeding through reading. When I was six, we moved to opposite the central library in Kirkcaldy. And that was where I began to understand that the world was much wider than Fife. It helped me to see the broader horizons and things I could aspire to do that weren't necessarily obvious from where I stood in my little town. It opened my imagination and my desire for exploration. I was looking for a place where I could be myself in the world.

"I personally didn't feel like I had a home in this country. And that is the thing that has changed so much. Now there is a place for me."

Although we've always been politically quite radical, Fife was in many ways socially quite conservative when I was growing up. In the Fife of the sixties, there were no lesbians. People were afraid and shy to be themselves. I grew up in my teens feeling like an outsider but not sure why. When I escaped and went off to read English at St Hilda's College, Oxford, I thought I would never come back. It was in Oxford, when I took classes about sexual politics and found feminist literary criticism, that my eyes were opened completely. In fact, it totally blew my mind. That led me to the feminists, and the feminists led me to the lesbians.

When I came back to Scotland in the late seventies, nothing had changed. It wasn't yet the place where I could live the life I wanted and just be myself. In the years before and during the debate over Section 28 [legislation banning the "promotion of homosexuality" by local authorities], I felt really uncomfortable a lot of the time. People would actually say things to me like "I don't want you to be in the same changing room as my wife" or "I don't want you near my children". The discussions and debates we have now about trans rights give me a shiver of recollection from that time.

I grew up thinking, this is my home, this is my country, but I don't belong here somehow. I personally didn't feel like I had a home in this country. And that is the thing that has changed so much. Now there is a place for me, and we also have a much more diverse society, which I'm so happy to see. We should embrace that. It doesn't matter who you are, the colour of your skin, what your sexuality is, whether you're neurodiverse or have a normal boring brain like me, there's space for all of us, and that can create a healthier society.

I think we all need a place where we feel we belong. Really that's what I was looking for in the wider world: a place where I could just be myself. I found that initially in Manchester; then I moved around for a while before coming back to Scotland. And, at that point, the country had changed dramatically. It wasn't the same place, and that was a great thing.

As is so often the case, love was the reason I decided to move back here. My partner is a professor at St Andrews, and I can write anywhere. But I also felt that the time was right. There was a lot of excitement in that as well. When we were considering moving back, I remember coming to visit, being unsure on the drive. But then I parked the car up here in the East Neuk and I saw the sea and everything in front of me, and I said to myself, "I think I'm in the right place."

ACKNOWLEDGEMENTS

The true heroine of this book is project manager Rachel Morrell, who arranged absolutely everything, conducted the interviews with great personal warmth and composed a first draft of each piece for me to work on.

I'm also grateful to the contributors themselves. They gave their time cheerfully and generously, and in sharing not only a cherished place but the stories and memories that made it so, will have greatly encouraged others.

Huge thanks also to photographer Susie Lowe, whose lovely images are themselves a place in which to lose yourself. Or find yourself, come to that.

Thank you to the copy-editing and layout team at Black & White; the mental health charity SAMH; the many agents, publicists and assistants who prioritised this project despite busy diaries and hectic schedules; my own literary agent Jenny Brown; and Friars Carse, Gleneagles and Cromlix Hotel for their hospitality.

Sally Magnusson

for Scotland's mental health

By buying this book you are supporting SAMH, Scotland's mental health charity.

We trace our roots back to 1923 with the groundbreaking work of Scottish psychiatrist Dr Kate Fraser. At a time when women were expected to remain at home and mentally ill people were routinely shut away in workhouses or prisons, Dr Fraser's dedication to improving the conditions and treatment of people with mental health problems was truly inspirational. We've been pioneering change ever since.

Our vision is a Scotland where anyone can ask once and get help fast. In 2022, we supported 25,000 people with their mental health and wellbeing. In addition to the SAMH Information Service, we operate over seventy community services across Scotland, ranging from mental health social care support to help with addiction, employment and more.

True to our origins, we continue to influence positive social change through our policy and campaigning work, nation-wide efforts in suicide prevention and physical activity, and our hosting of See Me and respectme, Scotland's anti-stigma and anti-bullying programmes.

It comes as no surprise that mental health and wellbeing appear as a recurring thread throughout this book. In choosing a perfect place, many of us will be led to locations where we have felt joy, discovered peace, forged treasured memories with loved ones or simply found solace in tough times. We are delighted that this includes an encouraging contribution from our ambassador, Sir Chris Hoy.

We hope you feel inspired by the stories that bring Scotland to life in these pages, which may even lead to your own journey. And by supporting SAMH, you will be empowering others to travel along the path to positive mental health and wellbeing.

Thank you.

Billy Watson
Chief Executive of SAMH